About Island Press

Since 1984, the nonprofit organization Island Press has been stimulating, shaping, and communicating ideas that are essential for solving environmental problems worldwide. With more than 1,000 titles in print and some 30 new releases each year, we are the nation's leading publisher on environmental issues. We identify innovative thinkers and emerging trends in the environmental field. We work with world-renowned experts and authors to develop cross-disciplinary solutions to environmental challenges.

Island Press designs and executes educational campaigns in conjunction with our authors to communicate their critical messages in print, in person, and online using the latest technologies, innovative programs, and the media. Our goal is to reach targeted audiences—scientists, policymakers, environmental advocates, urban planners, the media, and concerned citizens— with information that can be used to create the framework for long-term ecological health and human well-being.

Island Press gratefully acknowledges major support of our work by The Agua Fund, The Andrew W. Mellon Foundation, The Bobolink Foundation, The Curtis and Edith Munson Foundation, Forrest C. and Frances H. Lattner Foundation, The JPB Foundation, The Kresge Foundation, The Oram Foundation, Inc., The Overbrook Foundation, The S.D. Bechtel, Jr. Foundation, The Summit Charitable Foundation, Inc., and many other generous supporters.

The opinions expressed in this book are those of the author(s) and do not necessarily reflect the views of our supporters.

No One Eats Alone

No One Eats Alone

FOOD AS A SOCIAL ENTERPRISE

Michael S. Carolan

ISLANDPRESS

Washington | Covelo | London

ISLAND PRESS is a trademark of the Center for Resource Economics.

Library of Congress Control Number: 2016952383

⊕ Printed on recycled, acid-free paper

Manufactured in the United States of America
10 9 8 7 6 5 4 3 2 1

Keywords: food justice, sustainable agriculture, farmworkers, CSA (community supported agriculture), farmers market, food hub, farm-to-table, nose-to-tail, nutrition guidelines, soda tax

Table of Contents

Acknowledgments

No One Eats Alone was years in the making. When you work on something that long, especially on a project that takes you around the world, you become reluctant to take sole credit for what's really the product of a collaborative process. My name might appear on the book's cover and spine, but many people made this book possible. Here are a few of those others who helped make this book what it is. If you enjoy the book, applaud them also. If you don't, blame me and me alone.

Bruce Wexler. Author and father-in-law extraordinaire. His encouragement and support early on taught me the art—boy, is it ever—of writing a proposal.

Emily Davis. What can I say? "Thanks!" just isn't enough. Emily has given me hope about the future of the publishing industry. Emily, my editor, *still edits*. But even more than that: she helped craft sentences, even a few entire paragraphs. *No One Eats Alone* would not exist were it not for her; not as an Island Press book, anyway, and certainly not in the form it has taken. She has been a steadfast supporter of this project who refused to let it die. I am forever grateful.

James Hale. My graduate student and the person with whom I talk critical food scholarship more than with any other. Many of my ideas have been shaped by those discussions.

Mike Fleming. My copyeditor and the person who found a way to balance my desire to maintain a conversational narrative with the need to follow the by-the-book rules. Thank you for allowing me to say what I want, *how* I want.

Mom and Dad. Where did my interest in food come from? Right there. I grew up in a small town in rural Iowa, hometown population: 350. We had, and they still have, an acre-large garden. As children, my sister and I went around town in the summer with a wagon full of corn, selling it door-to-door. And as a family, over the summer we spent hours weeding, picking, canning, pickling, and freezing almost everything we grew. Thank you for that, even though I didn't appreciate those experiences at the time.

Nora, Elena, Joey. They put up with my highs and lows throughout the writing project. They put up with my travel, which regularly took me away from home for entire weeks at a time—Nora, I really owe you on that count. I hope projects like this will give our kids (Elena and Joey) some idea of what their dad does, as I know they'll never read my peer-reviewed articles, and would never willfully expose them to such torture.

I also want to thank the following institutions and professional networks that supported this project in their own unique ways: Colorado State University (USA); Korea University (Korea); Australasian Agri-Food Research Network; Otago University (New Zealand); University of Auckland (New Zealand).

I also owe a huge debt to all those who have lent their voices to this book, from those quoted directly to those not quoted but who shaped its arguments by allowing themselves to be interviewed. As noted in the text, this debt extends to hundreds, literally. Thank you, thank you, one and all.

Parts of this project were supported by the National Institute of Food and Agriculture (grant number COL00725) (under the title "Food System Resilience along the Front Range") and by the National Research Foundation of Korea (grant number NRF-2013S1A3A2055243).

Changing the Foodscape

In our fast-paced, fast-food culture, everyone seems to be eating alone—all the time. Americans report that they eat nearly 50 percent of their meals alone,[1] while more than 60 percent of office workers typically have lunch at their desks—a phenomenon so prevalent it has earned a catchy moniker: desktop dining.[2] So why do I claim that *No One Eats Alone?*

Every meal, whether enjoyed around the family dinner table or scarfed down over a keyboard, is connected to a multitude of people. For this book alone, I interviewed more than 250 individuals—that's almost the size of my hometown in rural Iowa—from six continents engaged in various aspects of food's life. There are flavorists, senior executives of Fortune 500 food firms, lobbyists, food importers, branding consultants, community development specialists, public health officials, dietitians, veterinarians, crop scientists, feedlot managers, politicians, indigenous peoples, and residents from various low-income, inner-city communities.[3] They, and many more, are all part of the story of food.

Yet how often do we interact with this diverse spectrum of people? When was the last time you ate strawberries with the person who picked them, or when was the last time you picked them alongside someone different from yourself? Or knew the name of the farmer who supplied your eggs? Or thought about how we can describe, with a straight face, certain foods as "healthy" even though they are made using processes that spoil the environment and exploit human beings—have you seen the working conditions that some farm laborers endure? What, precisely, is healthy about *that*?

Everyone who eats—that is, everyone—is affected by (which means they also affect) others in our vast foodscapes. I opt for the term *foodscape* instead of the more familiar *food system* because the latter is too narrow for what I have in mind, often reducing the life of food to a commodity chain—producers, processors, distributors, retailers, and consumers. The hows and whys of food are more complex than that, involving questions of power, culture, relationships, feelings, citizenship, and more.

Food is complicated because it can both connect and separate us. So why do we ignore these broken relationships as we struggle with dire problems such as obesity, climate change, malnutrition, and depressed rural economies? Perhaps because it's easier to blame an external enemy than to look within. In the modern food fight, our greatest adversary isn't underproduction, evil corporations, ignorance, or junk food. It's *us*. Us: thinking we can fix things without working together, even though the immensity of today's problems begs for a strategic, coordinated, and collective response. Us: believing we can shop our way to a world where food isn't a privilege but a right, even though the system we're hoping to change is the one dictating what we can vote for as consumers. Us: assuming the challenges we face can be solved with technological fixes, while the evidence overwhelmingly indicates that their roots are thoroughly social in nature.

How ironic, then, that the solutions we've been reaching for to get us out of this mess—food engineering, nutritional literacy campaigns, even local and slow food—risk propelling us deeper into disarray. And how frustrating! I'm not saying that we should just hug it out and all these afflictions will disappear. But right now we're rarely even within arm's length of others who populate our foodscapes. That needs to change— though, don't forget, I'm no less critical of local food than I am of global commodity chains. Intrigued yet?

Luckily, the battle over what's for dinner isn't going to be determined by who has the deepest pockets. If it were only about money: game, set, and match, Big Food. Campaigns like McDonald's "You Deserve a Break" ads or Coca-Cola's relentless branding with baseball and other all-American pastimes have been enormously successful. Studies show eaters believe McDonald's hamburgers taste better when they're in the restaurant wrapper. If we think comfort food comes in a package, and never think about how it got there, industry increases its bottom line and our collective well-being suffers.

This isn't the last time in this book you'll encounter the phrases *Big Food* and *status quo*. I may seem to be breaking the rule I set for my students: never universalize when writing about food. I am not. Think of these terms as heuristics—analytic constructs, even. I am less interested in trying to identify a bogeyman—Big Food is no more populated by "bad" people than are the alternatives. Rather, my goal is to understand how associations and encounters come together to produce certain feelings about food. Various organizations, politicians, and government agencies, some whom I name in the pages that follow, are unquestionably working hard to protect the status quo. But I found that even the most tough-minded executives rarely argue that the industrial foodscape is healthy. Instead, they are simply seeking success by following a conventional path, trafficking in the institutional, infrastructural, and cultural arrangements that give the status quo momentum. It is these arrangements, more than any particular group or individual, that we need to challenge.

No One Eats Alone is filled with stories of people who are doing just that—and thereby changing their relationship to food and to one another. There are CSAs (community-supported agriculture) where white suburban moms and Chinese immigrants work side by side, reducing social distance as much as food miles. There are entrepreneurs with little capital or credit who are setting up online exchanges to share kitchen space, simultaneously upending conventional notions of the economy of scale and fulfilling their own aspirations. There is Farm Hack, a community of farmers who trade information about building and repairing their own equipment, pushing back against the trend of ever-greater dependence on farm-implement manufacturers and technicians. There are parents and school board members who are working together to improve cafeteria food rather than relying on gimmicks like paying kids to eat their veggies or imposing soda taxes to combat childhood obesity. There are ranchers who, recognizing that animal health and human health are intimately linked, free-range their cattle rather than pumping them full of antibiotics, and who work to form connections with not-too-distant eaters to ensure that all the animal is used, not just the so-called select cuts—we forget that polycultures within the farm gate require polycultures beyond it. Alternative foodscapes like these don't have all the answers, but they do have one distinct advantage over Big Food: the connections made there stick.

It is my contention that these relationships are the key to healthy, equitable, and sustainable food. In other words, lasting social change requires, well, *social* change. This means that we need people to be politically active, which includes being involved in conventional forms of collective action. So write those letters to members of Congress, vote, and, if you are so moved, gather together to protest exploitive labor practices, runaway inequality, and the kind of corporate influence over food in our schools that has given rise to the claim that ketchup is a vegetable. But before eaters can be expected to engage in conventional forms of political resistance, they have to feel something for the often-distant others who populate our foodscapes and know that new worlds are possible by experiencing elements of them even before being able to articulate what they want. And in response to those who think the answers lie only with market forces, in shifting what we buy: *Radical change can occur only when people start acting like citizens first and consumers second.* Otherwise, we're left with "choice" that consists of Coke versus Pepsi.

Pointing to real-life examples, *No One Eats Alone* explores the wellspring of options that open up when citizen-eaters are nurtured. The following pages consist of what I call critical, hopeful storytelling: an account of what's possible when we work together.

CHAPTER 1

Monocultures of the Mind and Body

"You are what you eat." We have all heard this saying, and no doubt each of us has used it on a few occasions. Yet food is not only a *what,* but also a *when,* a *why,* a *how,* and a *with whom.* In other words, we cannot understand food without understanding the social practices that go along with eating and producing it, as well as all those activities that lie in between. Those practices have changed dramatically over the last half century, becoming far more homogenized, as illustrated in figures 1.1 and 1.2. Figure 1.1 tracks the narrowing dietary profiles of dozens of countries from 1961 to 2009, which also implies a narrowing of culinary skills, preferences, and knowledge. Figure 1.2 shows the same trends, focusing specifically on seven commodities, three industrial and four traditional.

How have we created these monocultures? Why have farming and eating patterns changed so much in such a relatively short period of time? And once new habits have become ingrained, how might they be changed again? Nutritional literacy campaigners would have us believe it's just as a matter of telling people what they ought to do and why. Easy-peasy. Next problem? But I'm afraid the roots of these monocultures run

Average change in the calories from crops in national diets worldwide, 1961–2009

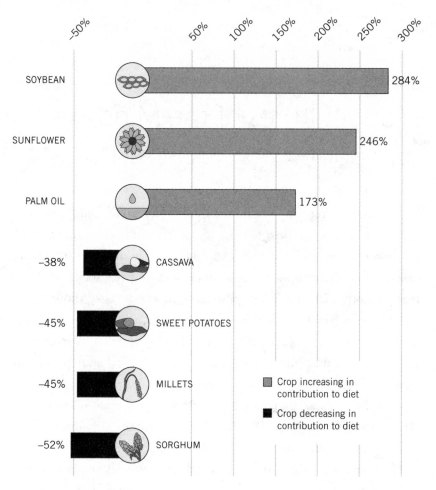

Percent change in calorie contribution to diet

−50% 50% 100% 150% 200% 250% 300%

SOYBEAN — 284%

SUNFLOWER — 246%

PALM OIL — 173%

CASSAVA — −38%

SWEET POTATOES — −45%

MILLETS — −45%

SORGHUM — −52%

■ Crop increasing in contribution to diet

■ Crop decreasing in contribution to diet

Source: Khoury et al. 2014. Proceedings of The National Academy of Sciences, USA.

FIGURE 1.1

Each country's food supply composition in contribution to calories in: ● 1961   ● 1985   ○ 2009

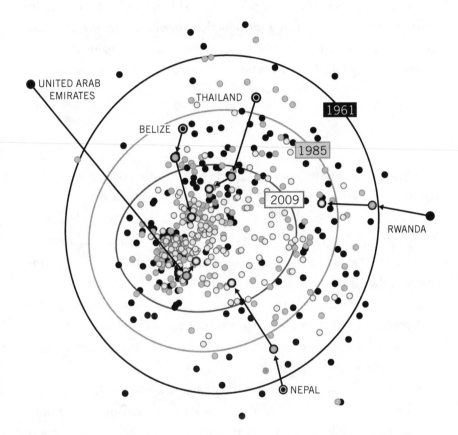

Source: Khoury et al. 2014. Proceedings of The National Academy of Sciences, USA.

FIGURE 1.2

too deep for our current course to be reversed by well-designed educational campaigns. To eat is to be connected, in one way or another. To eat differently, then, requires a change in those connections—that *social* change I talked about in the introduction. It will require places where people can come together, where they can develop new habits and feelings not only about food, but about each other.

It is a cold, rainy afternoon in The Hague. In other words, it is a typical January day in the Netherlands. I am seated across from a slender gentleman in his late sixties, though his athletic frame and jet-black hair, save for a light sprinkling of snow in his beard, give the appearance of someone at least ten years younger. George used to work for the Kenyan government in their ministry of agriculture, livestock, and fisheries. I wanted to learn more about Kenya's recent experiences with the global landgrab—companies and countries securing massive tracts of land in distant parts of the world for food and biofuel production. I had not expected us to get lost in a conversation about the Green Revolution. But after two hours and four coffees each, that was precisely what had happened.

The Green Revolution can be described as a series of research and technology transfer initiatives, with support from the Rockefeller and Ford foundations, that began in earnest immediately after World War II and lasted into the 1970s. I am also comfortable with the following definition, though it is not nearly as neutral sounding: the Green Revolution was the exportation of American-style conventional agriculture to lower-income nations, predicated almost exclusively on productivity gains—on producing, in a word, *more*.[1] From an environmental standpoint, the Green Revolution was at best highly problematic. At worse, it was an unmitigated disaster. To use Rachel Carson's metaphor, it single-handedly silenced spring around the globe, while making farmers and peasants dependent upon petrochemical inputs.

Take the case of wheat. New high-yielding dwarf varieties were bred short, hence the name. Varieties that are tall get easily flattened when subjected to high winds and significant rainfall. This, of course, is not a problem when the crop is harvested manually. When mechanically harvested, however, toppled wheat becomes fodder for field mice and rot, as the combine's head—the business end that pulls the plant into the machine—cannot get to it. Dwarf varieties not only stand up better to the elements than their taller cousins, they also make more sense when breeding for yield. To put it simply, tall plants waste energy getting tall. Shorter varieties make more efficient use of energy, when *efficiency* is defined by a plant's yield relative to the nutrients it absorbs. Yet paradoxically, this efficiency came at the expense of energy—a lot of it, once you factor in petrochemical use. Dwarf varieties were so short they could not compete for sunlight with native weeds that, it turned out, were quite tall; after all, they had coevolved alongside the native wheat varieties for centuries. As a result, yields of "miracle wheat" were pathetic without the use of large amounts of fertilizers and herbicides.

The Green Revolution also led to the global cultivation of just a handful of crops. When we're looking to do things bigger and better, the tendency is to specialize—to take advantage of economies of scale. Trace the average Western diet back to the soil and you will find roughly ten plants.[2] Ten plants might not technically constitute a global mono-culture but it is awfully close.

George and I talked about the magic-bullet mindset of the Green Revolution and both the arrogance and outright ignorance that it embodied. How could industrialization be the single answer to sustainably—and justly, healthily, etc.—feeding the world? As for those who suggest viewing the Green Revolution as a short-term solution, a bridge to ultimately more-sustainable practices: now that it has been more than sixty years, precisely how long is the bridge? When a set of practices are tied to massive profits for powerful actors whose power is derived from those profits, it is naïve to suppose that economic and political influence will ever be willingly abdicated.

Most of my time with George, however, was spent discussing the other monocultures the Green Revolution helped bring forth. As George recalled,

> The 1960s were a magical time in my country. We were seeing per-acre maize yields increasing by more than 4 percent a year. I believe that surpassed what they were even seeing in the US at the time. It was also a period of great structural change. The entire farm sector was undergoing immense transformation, starting to look a lot like the US Corn Belt. But also, and this is why I used the term "magical" earlier, we were forgetting some things that, in hindsight, we shouldn't have.[3]

Intrigued by his curious choice of words, I asked if he was implying that the Green Revolution was an act of collective forgetting.

"That's precisely what it was," he agreed. "We failed to appreciate, until after it was gone, the unique expert systems our ancestors had developed. I'm talking about knowledge that allowed them to grow food not only under remarkably adverse conditions, but to also do so sustainably, without the need of expensive nonrenewable resources, as in the case of fertilizers, or scare resources, if you're talking about irrigated water."

Later in the conversation he talked more specifically about how this social amnesia affects Kenyans today: "Looming threats from peak oil and water and from climate change make me wish we had done a better job saving that knowledge, because we're going to need it. If not now then very soon. The Green Revolution robbed us of a very important aspect of our past."

"Robbed of our past" might seem like a rhetorical flourish, but I caution against dismissing these words. For me, they immediately called to mind something that another George, George Orwell, expressed nearly seventy years ago. In his deeply unsettling and arguably prophetic dystopia, *1984*, he wrote, "Who controls the past, controls the future: who controls the present controls the past."[4] Sociologist Paul Connerton essentially makes the same point in *How Societies Remember*, noting that: "All totalitarianisms behave in this way: the mental enslavement of the subjects of a totalitarian regime begins when their memories are taken away." He continues by explaining, "What is horrifying about a totalitarian regime is not only the violation of human dignity but the fear that there may remain nobody who could ever again bear witness to the past."[5]

I can guess what you are thinking. Totalitarianism? Orwellian dystopias? Is that not a bit over the top? How could those things ever be linked with the Green Revolution? After all, wasn't Norman Borlaug, generally recognized as the father of the Green Revolution, awarded the Nobel Peace Prize, the Presidential Medal of Honor, and the Padma Vibhushan, Indian's second-highest civilian honor, for his work in developing high-yielding dwarf wheat varieties?[6] True, but remember this: those awards were for what the Green Revolution allegedly gave the world, not for what it took away. Calculate those subtractions, and a case could be made that, on the whole and over the long run, more was *lost* as a result of this "revolution" than gained.

But how? How can entire societies be stripped of the ability to bear witness to the past? More to the point, how is the Green Revolution implicated as a source of amnesia? The *how* is nothing mysterious—it's just the opposite, in fact. It's routine. And I mean that in the most basic sense of the word.

Michael Polanyi, the brilliant twentieth-century polymath, famously proclaimed, while discussing what he called the "tacit dimension": "We know more than we can tell."[7] Anecdotally, we all know this to be true. Ever try telling someone how to ride a bike? Or take that special dish your grandmother used to make for family occasions—for me that was the kolache. Asking her to write out the directions, with the addendum, "I want it to taste just like yours," never seems to work. Why? Because the knowledge required cannot be reduced to words. A great deal of our understanding is of this "more than we can tell" variety. Such a realization may seem trivial when compared with the practical hard work being done by scientists, activists, and practitioners to build healthier foodscapes. But this insight holds immense practical consequence. Until we give tacit knowledge its proper due, our food system cannot be transformed. If reformers hope to mount a serious challenge to the status quo, they will need to appreciate those aspects of food that are felt, practiced, and performed. To know something, in many cases, we have to *do it*, literally.

Consider that the world's biodiversity "hotspots," regions with the planet's richest collections of plants and animals, are also cultural and linguistic hotspots. An article published in the prestigious journal of the National Academy of Sciences reports that 70 percent of all languages left on the Earth are spoken in these biodiverse areas.[8] Coincidence? Hardly.

Virginia Nazarea, professor of anthropology and director of the Ethnoecology and Biodiversity Lab at the University of Georgia, is perhaps the world's foremost authority on the subject of biocultural diversity. Along with the late Dr. Robert Rhoades she helped pioneer research in this field. One of the many subjects she has studied in her illustrious career is sweet potato farming in the Philippines.[9] I am particularly struck by one study involving two sites. On one, farmers were beginning the processes of commercializing production for the market, while the other remained firmly at the level of subsistence agriculture to feed local households. As was expected, she witnessed a narrowing of genetic diversity on the site moving toward commercial production. Yet that was not all. There was also a large disparity between the two sites in terms of the number of varieties known or remembered, compared with the biodiversity that actually existed. At the commercial site, farmers had knowledge about far fewer sweet potato varieties than at the other (and no doubt they also had an even further eroded working knowledge, though this wasn't investigated), having forgotten many that still existed and were being planted elsewhere in the country. This suggests a faster erosion of cultural knowledge than of genetic diversity itself. Nazarea writes: "In the context of agricultural development and market integration, knowledge may actually be the first to go."[10]

That is the forgetting that George was alluding to. As crops and management practices stop being used, they risk being forgotten. As for conventional gene and seed banks, they are not saving nearly enough. What good is a seed once it is divorced from the people who cultivated it? Can you tell by looking at a seed how deep it ought to be planted or how it responds to certain weather? What about the taste, texture, and mouthfeel of the fruits it will bear? And how it ought to be harvested? Can you get any of this by examining a DNA sequence? I will let George answer those questions for me: "We had such incredible agro-biological diversity a half century ago [in Kenya]. The Green Revolution took that away from us. And now, because most everyone's dead who had a working knowledge of those alternative systems, it's proving difficult to reconstruct them, even though we have many of the seeds locked safely away in a seed repository."

And taste, how does that fit into this conversation? Does it matter whether we all like the same thing or have a variety of tastes? *Yes!*

Nazarea documents how differences in sweet potato preferences in the Philippines helps sustain the crop's diversity there.[11] Elsewhere, researchers mapping the wide genetic variability of corn landraces— locally adapted variations—in Mexico note that most will survive only so long as the country's culinary diversity remains intact and continues to require all those different varieties.[12]

We have already discussed how the Green Revolution helped reduce biodiversity at the production end, through farmers' collective forgetting. But we also forget as eaters. As tastes for certain dishes are lost, so too are the requisite skills to prepare them—which, by the way, further erode knowledge at the production end. If no one is eating a particular food, what's the point of growing it? Recall the earlier figures noting the global narrowing of diets. This forgetting isn't a possibility. It's well under way.

"I'm seeing an entire generation of young Africans," George explained, "those in urban areas especially, that eat very differently from past generations. I worry about how those habits will further erode an already perilously brittle food system." To illustrate his point, George went on to talk about a favorite dish of his: matoke—steamed plantains, essentially. "You can't make it with the bananas you find in Western grocery stores. I once tried using really green ones and it didn't come out right. You need plantains." He continued, "I don't see plantains disappearing anytime soon, but that's not my point. My point is that when we lose a taste for a dish we risk losing the plants, possibly forever, that make that food possible."

I interviewed Mick at his home in Kensington, a well-known and rather affluent district in central London. Mick retired from "the food biz," as he called it, in 2006, after spending forty-six years "making people want food from either a tin or a box." "The strategy has changed," he told me. "Fifty years ago half of our customers still knew how to cook. So early on I was working on [advertising] campaigns that were about trying to talk people out of cooking, telling them about how a certain product could save them time for other things, that sort of thing. We don't do that anymore because those cooking skills have been nicked."

"'Nicked'?" I asked.

"Right. Let me put that another way. *Lost* would have been a better term. But what that term doesn't convey is the intentionality of it. Back in the sixties and seventies we were really working to make that happen, to make it so people actually forgot how to cook, which is why my instinct was to say 'nicked,' or what you might call 'taken.'"

The Green Revolution has helped us forget how to grow and save the seeds of heritage fruits and vegetables. But that is only half of it, as we are also forgetting how to prepare and, in some cases, even eat certain foods. Who among us knows how to carve a turkey anymore? It's a slippery slope. The less we know about cooking the less cooking we do, which leads to knowing still less, doing still less, and so forth, until we have no "choice" but to eat only certain foods, like those that have already been prepared for us. Then there's the point of no return: after a generation or two, societies will not even know they have forgotten anything as entire cohorts are born into this new normal. As the old saying goes, *How are you supposed to know what you're missing if you don't know you're missing it in the first place?*

The long-game strategy articulated by Mick has paid off handsomely. And yet, for whatever reason, Mick showed both a readiness for reflection as well as contrition. "Mind you, at the time, starting out, I didn't think about what it really meant to make people so entirely dependent on food cooked by companies. But in hindsight it's now so very obvious: once companies started cooking it was only a matter of time before people, and before you know it entire generations, lose the ability to do something our ancestors took for granted. I do feel bad about having played a role in that." A few moments later he remarked, "It's not rocket science, learning how to grow, harvest, and prepare food. But even so, the skills most have for eating food basically extend to knowing how to run a can opener or, even worse, roll down their window on their old banger [car] while getting takeaway."

Mick's comments are important, as they cut the legs out of the argument that *eaters* are to blame for the kind of food industry produces: it's just good ol' supply and demand. Executives justify investment into highly processed food—heat and treat, or even better, grab and go— with the defense that they're just following consumer demand. Damn, lazy consumers! Eaters undoubtedly do buy these foods. But Mick's point is that we can't confuse *buying* those foods with *choosing* them. In many cases, eaters buy them because they *have* to, thanks to the efforts of individuals like Mick. "You have to appreciate the challenge faced by food companies, which is unique to them and them alone," he told me. "Unlike cars, or shoes, or tools, people can only eat so much. There's a limit to how much food you can get a consumer to buy, a ceiling that doesn't exist for other commodities—just look at how many shoes the average person owns." And yet, food firms populate the Fortune 500 list. The trick for maximizing profits, according to Mick, is to "find ways to steer people to buy products with higher [profit] margins, like ready-to-eat foods, an end aided considerably by consumers not knowing how to cook for themselves."

When eaters buy highly processed foods, I am reluctant to call it "choice." For many, it's dependence.

More than one livestock producer has told me that current food policy "maximizes assholes per acre." I appreciate this off-color phrase as it emphasizes what ought to be obvious: that livestock intensification maximizes *all* elements of animal production, even those for which there may be no market. I calculate that there are roughly 50 billion animals in our food system at any given moment: 45 billion chickens/ turkeys/ducks, 1.7 billion sheep/goats, 1.3 billion cattle, 1 billion pigs, 0.16 billion camel/water buffalo, and 0.12 billion horses.[13] That is a lot of "undesirable" meat—50 billion hearts, 100 billion eyeballs, and well over 100 billion feet.

Consider the American turkey tail: a case of one segment of the US poultry industry quite literally sticking its asses in the face of another nation's eaters. I mention it because it offers insight into how new foods become not so new—perhaps even becoming a "traditional dish"—and how much work must go into dislodging them when this happens.

The turkey's hind end, which also goes by such irreverent names as the parson's nose, pope's nose, or sultan's nose, is not all feathers, as many first presume. Turkey tails contain flesh, with about seventy-five percent of their calories coming from fat. If you are reading this in an affluent country you likely have never come across turkey tails in a retail setting. They remain a largely undesirable by-product of the poultry industry in most Western nations, even though roughly 230 million turkeys, and tails, were raised in the United States in 2015.[14] Not long after World War II, US poultry firms began dumping turkey tails, along with chicken backs, into markets in Samoa. (Not to single out the United States, New Zealand and Australia are on record for having done the same thing with mutton flaps—sheep bellies—to the peoples of the Pacific Islands.[15]) By 2007, the average Samoan was consuming more than forty-four pounds of turkey tails every year.[16] That is quite the success story for a food product "that was essentially nonexistent sixty years ago," to repeat what I was told by someone who grew up in Samoa in the 1930s and '40s.

Based on what I have learned from meat traders in New Zealand, Australia, and the United States, animal protein was historically scarce and so was considered to be a luxury among Pacific Islanders. Following

World War II, traders keyed in on importing meat products to this part of the world, even very low-quality cuts, given their desirability. It made alchemists out of entrepreneurs, as they were essentially turning waste into gold, or at least into American dollars.

Cheap food like turkey tails began displacing traditional foods, as the latter became more costly than imports and more time-consuming to prepare. So successful was this process of gastronomic integration that, over a generation or two, foods like duck tongue, turkey tails, and chicken feet began to be viewed not as foreign but as part of local cuisine. In the words of Becca, the Samoan quoted earlier who has since relocated to the United States, "If you were to interview my great-nieces and nephews [who still live in Samoa] and ask them to name a traditional Samoan dish, I bet some would answer by saying Budweiser and a barbecued turkey tail." Turkey tails are also common street food throughout the Pacific Islands, making them an important source of income for many lower-income families.

"Their integration," as Becca went on to explain, "has been so effective in part because of how we eat these foods." The *taste* of these foods, it turns out, cannot be uncoupled from feelings of conviviality, friends, and family. Again Becca: "Turkey tails are rarely eaten in isolation. They're eaten with friends and family, and, as I said earlier, often with something like a cold Budweiser in your hand. Even when you do eat it alone, if you get one on the street from the vendor, it's during your downtime. You don't eat turkey tails at work. You always eat them in moments of relaxation."

There are a number of important lessons to be learned here. For instance, we have in the turkey tail a story of a once-foreign food becoming, with time, a national delicacy imbued with a deeply felt sense of companionship and comfort. When this happens, it becomes trickier to get people to eat less of it, as public health officials are learning when it comes to the turkey tail. Changing dietary patterns requires more than just nutritional education. Pacific Islanders know it is not the healthiest food choice. Yet many still choose it. Banning the food does not work either. They tried that in Samoa, and a black market quickly emerged to satisfy demand.

Becca, I learned, does not care for turkey tails anymore, even though she claimed to have "loved them" when she was younger, before she emigrated to the United States. When I asked her what changed, she acknowledged that it wasn't education. She always knew that turkey tails were unhealthy: "I think all Samoans know that deep down. And yet still they eat it." So what caused her to turn away from a food she had deeply enjoyed? Leaning back in her chair she cast her gaze upward for a couple of seconds, searchingly. "I guess you could say I went cold turkey," she laughed. "They're harder to find here, for one thing. But now I can't stand them. The texture especially turns me off. The grease, the fat—it just doesn't feel right in my mouth."

While making those last remarks, her face changed. Tongue out, a frown: the look of disgust. Her aversion clearly went beyond the physical sensation of taste described by sensory scientists. And its roots extend well beyond the reaches of nutritional literacy campaigns. "Since moving to the States I have created new memories around new foods," Becca volunteered. "When I get together with friends we're not eating turkey tails or duck tongues, so I don't have those strong sentiments toward the foods, either, which I think also makes them less appealing. My new taste preferences reflect the new reality I inhabit, not something from back in my childhood. I left that behind years ago."

I have found few, flavorists included, who dispute that we taste with our entire bodies. We have long known, for example, the role the nose plays in taste, thanks to the scent receptors that detect thousands of volatile chemicals that give foods their "complexity"—what is known as orthonasal (front door) and retronasal (back door) olfaction. More recently, it was learned that the cells lining the small intestine also contain taste receptors.[17] When these intestinal sensors detect sugar, for instance, they trigger a cascade of hormones that ultimately ends with a little extra dose of insulin in the bloodstream. Yet, the embodied and therefore societal—as bodies do not exist in social vacuums— nature of taste goes even further than this. Sensory scientists might not always be tuned in to this reality. Food companies, however, most certainly are.

To quote Barb, a ten-year veteran in advertising who has worked for numerous major food firms: "Why do you think places like McDonald's have playgrounds in their restaurants or encourage that milestones like birthdays be held there? It's all about eliciting positive sentiments and memories. If you can give people a positive eating experience, it almost doesn't matter what the food tastes like. I mean, it does, but if the experience is strongly positive it [the taste of the food itself] doesn't matter nearly as much as if the experience was negative or neutral."

Memory can be incredibly powerful. I have a friend who cannot stomach pancakes because that was what he was eating as he watched the Twin Towers fall on that fateful September day in 2001. He learned the next day of the death of his uncle, trapped in the second tower. He tried eating pancakes again about two years ago. The smell alone left him in an uncontrollable, shirt-soaking sweat. He threw them away, batter and all, before the first one was finished cooking.

When I ask audiences for a show of hands from those who can link a food to a negative memory, and who in turn now avoid that food, the majority reach for the sky. In most cases the negative memory has to do with eating (or drinking) something, or too much of something, and immediately getting sick—my hand's going up right now. I once

OD'ed on shrimp in high school and haven't been able to stomach the food since. Audiences can also recall positive associations with food, but it usually takes them longer. Perhaps the links are harder to recollect precisely because they are so ubiquitous. A lot of what we eat is eaten because of positive associations. That was how Becca described the pull that members of her family in Samoa feel toward turkey tails, as a tug of conviviality and the warm glow of fond memories.

For a more systematic, and sustained, attempt at making a food feel good, take Coca-Cola's big bet on the power of positive sentiments: a technique that plays no small part in making the brand the global juggernaut that it is.

The onset of World War II weighed heavily on Coke executives. They knew that it was only a matter of time before the United States became embroiled in the conflict. The Great War was also still fresh in their minds. As the largest consumer of granulated cane sugar in the world by 1919, Coke was devastated by sugar rationing during World War I. Not wanting history to repeat itself, the company embarked on a mission to convince the US government that Coca-Cola was essential to the war effort. A nonalcoholic beverage, Coke was presented to government officials as something commanding officers could give to their troops without diminishing combat readiness. In the spring of 1941, Robert W. Woodruff, the company's president at the time, received a wire sent by an American reporter in London: "We, members of the Associated Press, cannot get Coca-Cola anymore. Terrible situation for Americans covering Battle of Britain. Know you can help. Regards."[18] There, in black and white, was his argument to the US government: Coca-Cola boosted morale. After the bombing of Pearl Harbor in December 1941, Woodruff announced the company's wartime policy: "We will see that every man in uniform gets a bottle of Coca-Cola for five cents wherever he is and whatever it costs."[19] Woodruff knew the long-term benefits of such a strategy even if the company lost money during the war. This was about more than getting people "hooked" on a particular soft drink. It was about creating an indelible brand: forever associating Coca-Cola with patriotism, freedom, democracy, and the liberation of millions from the Axis shadow.

Woodruff was decades ahead of everyone else in understanding the power of the taste experience. Coca-Cola's strategy was to get a Coke into the hands of people when they were happy—what, inside the company, is called the "ubiquity strategy." And recognizing that this is not always possible, as adults occasionally prefer drinks of a fermented nature, they focused on at least getting the product into the hands of children. Thus began Coke's long partnership with America's pastime, baseball. Now you will find Coke just about anyplace that elicits positive sentiments: sporting events, carnivals, zoos, concerts, McDonald's PlayPlace birthday parties. . . .

Barb, who also counts Coca-Cola among her past employers, points to how these strategies literally changed the taste of the product: "That's why people rate Coke as better tasting when they know it is a genuine Coca-Cola that they are drinking. The formula in an unlabeled Coke and a labeled one are identical. And yet people overwhelming rank the latter as better tasting. Those findings drive the flavorists crazy." It's true: studies confirm that consumers rate the taste of Coca-Cola higher when they know what they are drinking.[20] Related research has also been conducted with McDonald's french fries, chicken nuggets, hamburgers, milk, and apple juice: children consistently prefer the taste of those presented in McDonald's packaging over those served in a plain-white wrapping.[21]

When I talk of eaters—and growers too—feeling a *pull* toward certain foods, I'm not reaching for a metaphorical flourish. Deeply felt visceral reactions are at play. If a food is wrapped in fond memories and overlaid with cultural sentiments, don't expect a food literacy campaign to change anything. I know that deep-fat-fried cheese curds are about as healthy as methamphetamine. Even so, sentiments running back to my childhood, coupled with my continued identification as "a Midwesterner" (I'm from northeastern Iowa, where this dish is practically its own food group), would prompt my protest if anyone sought to ban its consumption.

This is also why I am encouraged. Granted, if memories, in the broadest sense, matter, then we cannot expect change to happen overnight. But that is not to say a food revolution is out of reach. The status quo can be disrupted if we do the work to put new memories in place. That is what the more successful alternative foodscapes are doing: growing from the ground up, one memory at a time.

Telling or teaching—two sides of the same coin, if you ask me—a person to eat differently assumes an oversimplified view of food. Food bans and food shaming: these are practices that rest on little more than wishful thinking. I should also note that such acts are culturally insensitive. Attempts have been made to ban turkey tails in Samoa, and I am sure some nutritionists would love to see similar actions taken on the "curds and beer" combo popular among many of my cheesehead friends back in Iowa and, especially, nearby Wisconsin. But those restrictions ignore the deeply social reasons why certain groups eat these foods. It is not about food addiction so much as it is about cultural reproduction. To eat these foods is to be connected. To eat differently, then, we have to encourage different connections. That is what the alternative foodscapes described in the following chapters are doing: building new communities.

CHAPTER 2

Knowing Quality

A Google search for nineteenth-century cookbooks returns many pages of results, all now in the public domain. It's a virtual time machine for anyone who wants a sense of how our ancestors experienced food. Among my favorites: *The White House Cook Book*, from 1887. The opening pages read: "To the wives of our Presidents, those noble women who have graced the White House, and whose names and memories are dear to all Americans, this volume is affectionately dedicated."[1] After dispensing with such formalities, the author transitions to practical advice about preparing a chicken dinner:

In choosing poultry, select those that are fresh and fat, and the surest way to determine whether they are young is to try the skin under the leg or wing. If it is easily broken, it is young; or, turn the wing backwards, if the joint yields readily, it is tender. When poultry is young the skin is thin and tender, the legs smooth, the feet moist and limber, and the eyes full and bright.[2]

Another illuminating read is *The American Home Cook Book*, from 1864. (The author's pen name alone speaks volumes about the times: "by An American Lady.") The book instructs the reader, when choosing lamb, to "observe the neck vein in the fore quarter, which should be of an azure-blue to denote quality and sweetness."[3] Or when selecting venison, "pass a knife along the bones of the haunches of the shoulders; if it smell [sic] sweet, the meat is new and good; if tainted, the fleshy parts of the side will look discolored, and the darker in proportion to its staleness."[4]

Azure-blue neck veins? Sweet-smelling haunches? Moist chicken feet? Eyes that are full and bright? What world did these people live in? I ask only partially in jest. Our ancestors did live in a different world, one whose inhabitants felt very differently about food than we do today.

Understanding what constitutes fresh, high-quality food cannot be separated from eaters' social environments. For some, these qualities are represented by "best by" dates, the feel of cans, or the look of produce. For example, are the tomatoes large and red? And the ears of corn—do they have signs of once harboring corn borers? For others, "knowing quality" looks and feels radically different, involving phenomena such as the color of neck veins, the smell of haunches, the cloudiness of eyes, and the elasticity of skin. Can you differentiate between the sound of a cantaloupe, when solidly whacked with a forefinger, that is immature (*thd*), ripe (*thud*), and well past its prime (*thhhuuuud*)? If not, I doubt you feel comfortable growing your own, as that would place the burden of knowing when to harvest squarely on your inexperienced shoulders. People without that kind of practical knowledge may be less inclined not only to garden, but also to shop at a farmers' market, join a community-supported agriculture (CSA) program, or participate in other efforts to *do* food differently.

Like Kim, from Kansas City, Missouri, who told me the "primary reason" she doesn't visit farmers' markets or belong to a CSA is because she has "no idea how to pick out fresh foods without a sell-by-date sticker." Or Larry, from Omaha, Nebraska, who told me about his kids who think "fruits and vegetable have to look flawless if they're going to eat them—not the ideal disposition if we were to suddenly start getting food from local organic growers, or our own backyard." Or Paul, from London, who told me about how he "can't stomach going to the butcher's because of the smell." "The meat *smells* there," he told me, as if reporting late-breaking news. And yet, it is precisely *because of* that smell that others are drawn into these establishments. To quote Beverlyn, another Londoner, who regularly frequents her neighborhood butcher shop: "I need to smell my meat if I'm going to buy it. Otherwise, how do I know it's fresh?"

If all we understand are the qualities of Big Food, then don't expect a food revolution anytime soon. The moment we begin reorganizing our communities and social networks, however, those qualities become open to change. Then, anything is possible.

I first met Kurt at an open-air food market in Melbourne, Australia, while interviewing sellers and buyers from this space—a space, coincidently, full of cantaloupes needing a good "thudding" and poultry with exposed wings, for turning, and skin, for pinching. We had a small-world moment, discovering that our roots extend to rural Iowa, where we were both born. Kurt is an advertising executive for a major firm in Brisbane. After this serendipitous introduction, Kurt agreed to meet me two days later in his office for a proper interview. When we finally did sit down for that talk, the subject quickly turned to those ubiquitous, and all-too-confusing, "sell by," "best before," and "for maximum freshness eat by" labels.

"Processed foods by nature take a lot of the thinking out of the eating process," he explained. "You're not supposed to think about whether it's safe. Ideally, if it's on the store shelf it's safe. Period."[5] Kurt went on to explain how this is what consumers want. "That's part of the value-added of processed foods; not having to judge, other than by reading something like a 'sell by' label." I heard that a lot, from Kurt and others: consumers want to read more about why their food is safe, though (as noted in the prior chapter) reading is only one way we know food. *How we know* shapes *what we feel* for things, which ultimately produces a pull toward certain foodscapes. Here's a rather stark example of how knowing, feeling, and being come together: I have had more than a few people admit to not gardening at least in part because they wouldn't know when to pick what they have grown. This confession led one to half-jokingly add, "If vegetables grew with best-by dates, I might feel differently about acquiring a green thumb."

Like Mick in the prior chapter, Kurt acknowledged the value of this reliance for creating market share. "It doesn't hurt that they [referring to phenomena like best-by and sell-by labels] make consumers dependent upon us and our labels." Grinning, he continued, "That's something that gives us a distinct market advantage over these more-local supply chains. People nowadays need food with their ingredients listed and their various labels and 'sell by' dates." He then sat up and leaned forward. Putting his elbows on the desk between us—one of those I'm-going-to-let-you-in-on-something postures—his voice dropped a level, as if divulging a secret. "I've always encouraged my clients to list everything on their packaging. Consumer surveys tell us that this is what consumers want; they want to read about their food. And, frankly, the more they feel like they need these things the less they'll feel comfortable getting their foods through unconventional channels, like open-air markets, street vendors, or directly from farms."

Secret or not, Kurt is correct. The evidence indicates that, "regardless of gender, race, age, location, income group, educations level, or shopping venue," the vast majority of "consumers place a very high degree of importance on the issue of produce safety," to quote one study on the subject.[6] But that by itself does not tell us much. Of course people want to eat food that is safe. More interesting is *how* consumers grasp food safety, something that, for many eaters, is more explained than experienced, which is to say it is conveyed more through words and dates than through an engaged knowledge that cannot be reduced to terms, other than superficially. For example, you can tell someone about the virtues of sweet-smelling shoulder meat, but until they have experienced it they would not have a clue what to look for, or smell for, the next time they're at the butcher's shop. Forget about azure-blue neck veins and moist chicken feet. What do the words on the packaging say? That is what many of today's eaters are primarily interested in when it comes to food safety, and Big Food wouldn't want it any other way.[7]

Kurt understands the long-term ramifications of this particular grasp of food quality. You might even say he has made a living at trying to make sure eaters do not know good food by any other way. He acknowledges that dependence on sell-by dates, labels, and the like directly "translates into greater profits for my clients and my firm."

Among industry insiders, Kurt's sentiments were fairly typical. Numerous others spoke of how eaters' understanding of phenomena like quality and safety—"if pitched right," to quote Marcy, whom you will learn more about in a second—played right into the hands, and deep pockets, of firms. Marcy holds an executive-level position within a well-known international food company. A food scientist by training, Marcy has held positions in advertising, public relations, and human resources before landing a second-in-command position for one of the company's many divisions.

"We've conditioned consumers to think about issues like food safety and freshness as they would a Twinkie." Marcy then asked how I would determine if a Twinkie was fresh.

Not wanting to lead the conversation, I answered with a question: "Fresh as in 'just packaged' or fresh as in 'edible'?"

"That's my point," she said. "We've gotten so good at having food looking like it's just off the vine or the tree or just off the factory line with the Twinkie—we've genetically engineered apples to be cut into and *not brown*, for Christ's sake!" She added, "It's all about the visuals. The 'best by' date stamped on the box. Has the box been opened? Or the individual wrapping, it is still intact? And the color, is it that classic golden brown?" (She is talking about Twinkies here.) "The more consumers rely upon those visuals to determine quality, the easier our jobs are for giving them products they want."

The more consumers rely upon those visuals to determine quality, the easier our jobs are for giving them products they want. Remember this point, about Big Food's attraction to visuals, due largely to the fact that this knowledge travels well. It doesn't hurt either that visual knowledge appears more amenable to capital, especially compared with other ways of knowing that require bringing people together—practice, practice, practice can't be easily bought. I cannot imagine an advertisement campaign educating people on how fresh poultry skin ought to feel, for example. That skill can only be acquired with practice, usually with the help of others who already have it. Alternative food networks are interested in visuals, too, in part so their food can effectively speak to eaters who haven't acquired this experiential feel for food quality. But their revolutionary potential lies in their ability to engender understanding that makes such heuristics as "undented can = good" and "it's-on-display-in-the-produce-aisle-so-it-must-be-fresh" wholly insufficient.

This leads me to my curious exchange with Robbie, a food scientist. "Seven out of ten consumers prefer number 33." Having spent roughly fifteen summers painting for my dad, who is a paint contractor (when not out in his garden), I immediately recognized what Robbie was holding: a color fan. But wait—we were just talking about salmon.

"Wild salmon gets its rich, pink color from its diet," Robbie continued. "Farmed salmon are on a completely different regimen, made up of chicken leftovers, soybeans, wheat, some corn—things you don't exactly find in a wild salmon's habitat. Nutritious and perfectly safe, but it also turns their flesh the same color as cod, that boring fishy grey."

Rarely does an interview go by where I don't regret a missed opportunity to press for an explanation, like this one about the nutritional value of farmed salmon. Truth is, the feed regime of farmed salmon *does* impact its nutrition profile. A 2016 study, for example, compared the fatty acid composition of over 3,000 Scottish Atlantic salmon farmed between 2006 and 2015, and found that, during that period, overall fat levels increased alongside a decrease in EPA and DHA ("good" fat) levels.[8] This has happened as marine-based feed—fishmeal and fish oil—are replaced with terrestrial ingredients that can be more cheaply raised and replenished, like soybean meal. "Consequently," as the authors note, "the nutritional value of the final product is compromised requiring double portion sizes, as compared to 2006, in order to satisfy recommended EPA and DHA intake levels endorsed by health advisory organizations."[9]

Grappling with why Robbie was holding a color fan, I failed to steer the conversation in this direction. Instead I blurted out, "Are you telling me you're able to order their flesh to color, with that number 33 being the most popular?"

"You got it," he answered, a little more matter-of-factly than I was expecting. With that he collapsed the fan, grasped it with one hand, and began waving it back and forth: "As they say, just pick a number!" Through our conversation I learned that salmon farmers feed their fish precise doses of the carotenoid pigments based on the color chosen.

"The research is clear, when selecting salmon it's all about color. What else do consumers have to go by? Most don't know how they're supposed to smell or feel. It's color or nothing."

While every generation is told from a very young age that beauty is only skin deep, we seem to forget to extend that adage to food. A study published a few years back offers a cautionary tale of what happens when we go chasing after good looks in the produce aisles. The vegetables that populate most grocery stores are anywhere from 5 to 40 percent lower in minerals—such as magnesium, iron, calcium, and zinc—than those harvested a half century ago.[10] Part of the reason can be traced to the dilution effect, bringing to mind another popular adage: bigger is not always better. Today's vegetables (fruits are less prone to this effect, save for perhaps the tomato) are often considerably larger than their ancestors, the result of years of breeding where a premium has been placed on heft. To quote Professor Harry Klee, a molecular horticulturalist and one of the world's leading tomato aficionados, "If you ask commercial seed companies why they are making tomato varieties that have lost all their flavor, the answer is very simple." He is quick to point his figure at commercial growers. "What does a grower get paid for? Yield, size, and appearance. They make more money for very large tomatoes than they do for small ones. The grower is not paid for flavor. So you have a fundamental disconnect between what growers want and what consumers expect."[11]

Supersized produce acquires its impressive girth by containing more dry matter, which dilutes mineral concentrations. Nearly 90 percent of this dry matter is carbohydrate. Consequently, as breeders select for high yield they are essentially selecting for fruit rich in starch with no guarantee that other nutrients and thousands of phytochemicals will increase in proportion to yield.[12] This is not news. Breeders have known about the dilution effect in produce for decades.[13]

Ironically, the very efforts to increase the production of fruits and vegetables that are pleasing to the eye have actually produced foods that are less nourishing—though nourishment has never been the primary aim of breeding. And, for that matter, neither has taste.

"That's the Holy Grail, breeding fruits and vegetables that are pleasing to the eye, that can withstand the brutalities of mechanical harvesting and transportation, that can ripen off the vine so they are not overripe by the time they land in the grocery store, and that also taste good." Through now retired, Sam spent the previous twenty years in various purchasing divisions of large food firms. In this role, he was responsible for sourcing major fast-food chains, soup companies, and grocery stores. Sam was quick to point out another unintentional artifact of breeding for looks—its impact on flavor. As he explained: "We're telling people to eat more fresh fruits and vegetables, but I think we need to be clearer about the types of fresh fruits and vegetables they ought to be eating. A lot of stuff out there just doesn't taste good. And I should know. I've tasted most of it."

He circled back to his Holy Grail comments: "Earlier, when listing off what breeders focus on, I listed taste last. That was intentional. If something doesn't handle transport well, is too delicate to be tossed around during harvest, then it doesn't make a bit of difference if it tastes amazing. It has zero value for a business. So when we tell people to eat more fruits and vegetables and they turn around and eat these beautiful but relatively flavorless things they've picked up at their grocer's produce aisle and, lo and behold, they don't like it—well, I'm just saying: we shouldn't be surprised they don't eat more fresh fruits and vegetables."

As I learned talking with breeders, it is actually very difficult to achieve both taste and durability with some produce, as each trait is premised upon opposing physiological and chemical characteristics. With the tomato, for instance, much of its taste and acidity is locked away in its locular jelly—that part of the fruit that my five-year-old recently called "goo." Breeders of industrial tomatoes, however, who are more interested in building in traits for harvest and transportation resiliency, concern themselves with the skin and pericarp—that structure between the skin and locular cavities. This explains why you need a steak knife to cut into some of them, and why the reward never seems worth the effort.

The quest for the beautiful, perfectly transportable tomato doesn't just negatively impact taste, or nutrition. How do you suppose these objects of beauty are able to maintain their appeal, even after traveling thousands of miles? Breeding has a lot to do with it. Yet anyone with a garden knows that the unblemished image on the seed pack is a one-in-a-million look. Rarely do the plants in and fruits from my garden look as perfect as the images that grace seed catalogs.

Take cucumbers. They can get partially buried in the soil, which turns the submerged part a perfectly harmless white. Still others are as curved as a severely arthritic finger, which could cause problems if I were hoping to pack and ship them long distances. After each harvest, large-scale cucumber farms routinely end up feeding to livestock or tilling back into the soil thousands of pounds of their vegetables due to these problems.[14] Bananas are vetted as if for a Hollywood casting call. Half of those grown in Australia are thrown away.[15] A good portion of this waste is the result of them not having the right shape. It was reported, for example, that more than 100,000 tons of Queensland bananas go to waste every year for not meeting cosmetic retail standards.[16]

Effie is in purchasing. She has the unenviable job of keeping the soup division of a major firm supplied. Soup can be a sourcing nightmare, given all the ingredients involved—tomatoes, carrots, onions, celery, corn, barley, and potatoes, to name just a few of the foods constantly on her mind. "Soup is the industry's answer to food waste. What do you think happens to the off-size vegetables, those that don't meet the standards for another division? They end up in your canned beef and barley or vegetable soup."

"*All* off-size vegetables?" I asked, though I knew the answer, having already interviewed numerous purchasers and large vegetable growers.

"No, not all," Effie confessed. She went on to tell me how the vegetables her company purchases fall into one of three boxes. "First, the just-right box—the vegetables you'd see in any produce aisle. Next, those with the right size but wrong shape or those that are too big. This box goes to us, for our soups, to make baby carrots, things like that. Then there's the too-small box. They're just too much work to do anything with. The farmer is stuck with them. They either end up being fed to pigs or they get tilled under. We won't take them."

They really don't have a solution to all food waste, I pointed out— not as long as they've got that last box, effectively a rubbish bin.

"Because customers expect produce to look a certain way, we can't just sell the off-sized directly to them," she admitted. "And the economics just doesn't work for us to handle the smaller stuff. It's cost-effective to push that cost back onto the farmer. It's all spelled out in their contracts. It's a common clause throughout the industry. Why should we eat a loss if we can avoid it?"

Effie's claim that this is common practice throughout the industry squares with what I have been told by others, including some of the farmers doing the "eating" of these losses. I mention this exchange to, first, highlight another cost (viz., waste) that comes with basing judgments about which foods to select on a particular visual aesthetic. It is also important to keep in mind *who* is disproportionately paying the costs. Food firms are structured to deflect these expenses. Picture yourself as a large-scale carrot grower. Assume that your contract with Campbell's Soup was not renewed (every carrot farmer I know of any significant scale is under contract). What would, what *could,* you do? It is not like you can take two tons of carrots to your local farmers' market and expect it all to sell. Bugs Bunny notwithstanding, no one likes carrots *that* much. You lack exit power, which is never a good thing. In such a situation, firms have leverage to extract concessions from growers. Or in Effie's words, they have the power to make farmers "eat" waste.

This drive for beauty is also costing the environment, though I can't image a situation where costing the environment doesn't also cost humans. Beyond resources wasted when food is discarded—a recent study calculated food waste in the EU translates into roughly 325 liters of water lost *per day for every individual* in the region—the annual cost of pesticides on human and environmental communities is staggering. In the United States alone, the yearly cost has been placed at roughly $10 billion.[17]

Chemicals have become so synonymous with productivity that we sometimes forget their role in aesthetics. Many pesticides are enlisted to keep our food looking just right. Even if I were to properly cage all my garden plants, keeping fruits and vegetables off the soil so they do not become discolored, I still have to contend with pests. It was not until elementary school that I learned that corn borers, which I like to refer to as the state of Iowa's unofficial invertebrate animal, were not an actual food. An exchange I heard often as a child, whenever sweet corn was served, went something like this:

Person 1: "There's a worm on my corn!"
Person 2: "Don't worry, it's just protein."

Most eaters today have no appetite for corn housing a harmless corn borer. Even the borehole—a trace of an organism long since departed—is unacceptable and has the power to evoke visceral disgust. We learn as children that cooties don't exist and yet we treat a sterilized hole (assuming the cob has been boiled) as if it were afflicted by this mythical pathogen. To combat the equivalent of food cooties we employ copious amounts of chemicals, something we should fear a lot more than harmless insects. This is not to suggest that insects don't eat crops. But the term "crop loss" is a misnomer. Often, crops said to be "lost" are not actually destroyed, as in nothing left. Plum curculio, a weevil known to feast on fruits throughout the Midwest, including plums, cherries, apricots, and other soft fruits, might poke a hole or two in an apple. The fruit remains perfectly edible. And yet, thanks to our aesthetic standards, the food, if sold through conventional supply chains, is deemed unsellable—lost.

"It took me a while to get over my aversion. My whole life, I only knew fruits and vegetables that looked a certain way. It was all based on ideal types—bananas that looked one way, and apples, tomatoes. I'm talking about their shape and size, but also whether they had any blemishes or bruising or bites taken out of them by insects." Lynn lives in Fort Collins, Colorado, a community about sixty-five miles north of Denver. Lynn, in her words, is "relatively new to the whole local food scene." She explained the root cause of what she called her "conversion" in the following terms: "Thanks to the recession, I decided to try growing my own food and it sorted itself from there." This conversion, however, did not occur overnight. "I had to figure out what to do with those fresh vegetables, for one thing. One thing that did happen pretty quickly was I realized I needed to recalibrate how I thought foods ought to look. Before long, I got used to eating foods that weren't perfect looking."

Interesting word choice: *recalibrate*. I wondered how far this process of recalibration went. Was this a tale of two worlds, an acceptance of flaws in the backyard garden and an ongoing expectation of perfection at the grocery store? I asked her, "Has this had any impact beyond the foods you eat from your garden?"

Her answer seems to indicate something deeper was afoot. "Sure it has. I really do avoid buying conventionally raised produce. I can't say I know for sure the pesticides, waxes, and other chemicals used in making foods look perfect are bad for us, though I suspect they are. Perfection comes with risks. You learn that when you get away from relying entirely on foods from long supply chains. I'd rather eat a slightly less attractive apple than a luminous red one, like the one from *Snow White*."

I've repeatedly encountered comments like this, about how eaters became recalibrated—I like that term (thanks, Lynn)—to alternative foodscapes, and through that process became more willing to make trade-offs that work against chemically dependent agrifood chains.[18] Those looking for perfection in the produce aisle want an assurance that their foods will be insect- and worm-free, but they're willing to take a chance on pesticide residue. Eaters like Lynn, however, value things quite differently. The guarantees they seek concern chemical-free food; the possibility of a corn borer lurking under the husk is viewed as an acceptable uncertainty—after all, it's just protein. I need not tell you which calibration Big Food is interested in maintaining.

Some hundred-plus years ago, industry faced the very problem that alternative foodscapes confront today. Eaters understood quality in a way that did not bode well for commercial wares and practices. The corporate response: expose consumers to information that could be readily *explained* (recall my earlier discussion about, for example, sell-by dates) in the hope they would forget those more *experiential* ways of knowing. The first generation is always hardest to convince, or perhaps

I should again use the term *recalibrate—convince* suggests the process is entirely based on reason and conscious calculation. My ninety-five-year-old grandmother, who can select poultry by looking at an animal's neck veins and skin, is accustomed to eating animals that entered her kitchen with a head, to paraphrase a view I have often heard her express. For her and others of her generation, "labels just don't tell you enough," to quote Leonard, my most senior interviewee, a ninety-eight-year-old World War II veteran from Auckland, New Zealand. For my generation, labels are commonplace and animal heads are alarming. Eaters like Leonard and Grandma have grudgingly come to accept these heuristics—like "good salmon = number 33 pink with a non-expired date"— that Big Food is peddling, though both admit to never having bought into them 100 percent. As Grandma once told me, "I know how to read expiration dates and I always feel for dents in cans before buying them, but I have always preferred the techniques we used for judging food when I was growing up." The "new normal" for one generation is just plain normal for those that come later.[19]

To fill in the knowledge gaps brought on by an increasingly industrialized foodscape, corporations offered consumers a steady diet of labels and advertisements—again, knowledge seeking to explain and even instruct: "Eat Fresh," "Think Outside the Bun," "Finger Lickin' Good," and "I'm Loving It," to offer a few contemporary examples from the fast-food industry. Some early food manufacturers, for example, concocted a "founder" and a "founding story" to help assuage consumer concerns about eating food without a face, as when W. K. Kellogg began placing his signature on each package of Kellogg's Corn Flakes. With the passage of the 1870 federal trademarks law in the United States, firms could protect images and narratives designed to act as proxies for the real-life experiences that previously informed eaters about their food. The Quaker Oats Man was "born" in 1877, followed by Aunt Jemima (1905), the Sweetheart of Corn (1907), the Morton Salt Girl

(1911), Betty Crocker (1921), and the Jolly Green Giant (1926). All were designed to put a face back on food, which had by then been removed by industrialization.

FIGURE 2.1

Early food packages also contained text—a ridiculous amount by today's standards. A representative image typical of the period can be found in the figure 2.1, a 1918 advert for Campbell's Soup. Apropos of Mick's comments from the last chapter, about cooking skills having been "nicked," the ad actually makes a case *against* home cooking. Companies reasoned that more text equaled greater reassurance, at least until eaters acquired their own stories and memories about these foods. That's why Campbell's ads today contain very few words but images of smiling faces and happy families. The goal is no longer to *convince* but to *remind* individuals why they ought to buy this particular brand of canned soup. Early on, eaters were so suspicious of packaged foods that they actually took the time to read these extravagant tales.

A century later, actors in alternative foodscapes are busy telling their own stories, but from the ground up.

Jack understood this well—the importance of telling eaters food stories that went beyond words or images. "I just can't sit back while people pluck stuff from my crates. The way I look at it, my job doesn't stop at just growing food. I want to get them excited about food. And to do that I need to be out there with them, showing them what a nice, fleshy, ripe tomato looks and feels like."

Jack is a farmer who sells fruits and vegetables at farmers' markets in and around Denver, Colorado. I joined Jack at one of these venues. He practiced what he preached. Having watched him closely, I can vouch that he sat only once during the entire event, when his three-year-old granddaughter came back with a bag of popcorn from a neighboring vendor and demanded to take a seat on his lap. Other than that, he was busy rubbing, poking, smelling, and shaking his produce, and instructing potential customers to do the same.

Later, while we were tearing down, I asked him about what I had observed. "This isn't just about selling my stuff; it's about selling *our* stuff," he said, at which point his arms went up in an "everyone here" gesture. A few moments later, as we were about to say our farewells for the day, he bent down and picked up an orphaned tomato that was resting by our feet. "This shouldn't have been picked. It has another week of maturing to do and I told a customer that. I want my customers to experience not only what a good tomato tastes like but also what it feels like. The feeling of ripeness is one of the first things our customers confront at the point of purchase, mind you, so we need to do a better job at prioritizing that."

He turned toward his Ford F-250 pickup truck and began to walk away, tomato in hand. Then he called back, "There's a bigger-picture purpose to all of this that we can't lose sight of. The more consumers understood our food, the less they'll feel comfortable with that crap at the store."

He reached his truck before turning. With his tomato-less hand he cupped his mouth and yelled, "It's a food revolution, man!"

CHAPTER 3
Shaping Values

Food writers generally avoid tramping into the thorny terrain of ethics. Remarkable, when you think about it. After all, a good bit of what we're fighting over when it comes to food concerns ethical claims. Eat this. Avoid that. Why? Because that is what you should do. For the environment! Because animals feel pain, too! Support local businesses! Food justice! There is no reason to be daunted by the subject of ethics, or *values*, a term I generally prefer because it seems slightly less esoteric. It is an utterly mundane topic, and I mean that with no insult to ethicists. Grappling with our values is not about casting our gaze skyward, but about creating the everyday human connections that evoke real empathy and understanding. "Buy local" starts to mean something more when you know the guy who owns and operates the neighborhood butcher shop. "Free-range" seems more important if you've visited a sustainable ranch or, on the other hand, if you've ever seen a battery cage up close. "Food justice" can move from being a politically correct platitude to a deeply felt commitment when you've worked alongside those whose station in life is different from your own. We need to start considering ethical claims at that level. We tend to preach what we practice, because through practice—what we *do*—certain ethical claims just feel right.

I met with Joe at his vacation home in Aspen, Colorado; the house was about twice the size of my permanent (and only) residence. Joe's a retired executive who spent more than thirty years working for various food firms, first in marketing as a graphic design artist, and finally as CFO—Chief Financial Officer. Hence that home in Aspen, which was, in his words, "a gift I treated myself to for my last promotion."

"Flavor, mouthfeel, that's all-important—don't get me wrong. But that's the easy part, making foods that are tasty." (That's not what food scientists and flavorists tell me, but I digress.) Joe continued: "People think things like advertising is about creating mindlessness: consumers who don't think and care about what they buy, who just buy what they're told. Truth is, we want consumers who think and care about what they buy. Marketing is ultimately about instilling within people a sense of care. A focused care, but for certain things nevertheless."

A focused care? Intrigued, I asked Joe for clarification.

He smiled, one of those hand-caught-in-the-cookie-jar grins that I see often on my children—I know it well. "Perhaps I've said too much, or at least I should have put it differently. Listen: food companies can do well when that sense of caring focuses on things like one's family, of being a good provider, feeding their family a healthy, affordable meal. When it starts involving things like a livable wage, that's not a conversation food companies want to get involved in, if they can help it. They don't want consumers thinking about that stuff when contemplating whether or not to buy their products." Joe is not simply explaining how food firms try to entice eaters with their advertisements, something we all know. He is also acknowledging that Big Food subtly, but very intentionally, socializes eaters to care about personal values, like being a good provider or responsible parent, and to keep the well-being of *others*, such as farm laborers or factory workers, tucked away in the shadows of consciousness.

This fits with research examining what people feel when eating at chain restaurants. These establishments go to great lengths to create convivial "family" experiences.[1] When you talk to people who eat there with their loved ones they frequently mention things that relate back to caring, to wanting to be a good mother, father, and grandparent. Back to Joe: "Like Olive Garden's 'When You're Here You're Family' campaign," which ended in 2013 after thirteen years, replaced with the slogan "We're All Family Here." He continued: "Sentiments attached to 'home,' 'family,' 'good parenting'—those sentiments travel well. Taste and food preferences might vary from one region to the next. The desire to be a good parent or grandparent, however— that's universal."

But let's be clear. Not just any sentiments that travel well will do. I would like to think that eaters are generally averse to human suffering. And yet, can you name an advertising campaign that zeroes in on hunger in Africa or pesticide poisoning in California when selling food? I can't, and I am sure I won't anytime in the foreseeable future.

Again Joe: "Look at McDonald's. Their ad campaigns, PlayPlace, parties—they've mastered this better than anyone. By making people care about things like 'family fun' [Joe makes air quotes with his fingers], they are able to make people forget about those other things that they have a poorer track record on, like the fact that the person taking their order may be on food stamps."

In any discussion of values, context matters immensely. Just ask the self-proclaimed "radical Earth First farmer" I interviewed, who admitted to taking his children to school in the family car recently during a blizzard, rather than using his bike, his usual method of transportation. "I know I shouldn't have done it. I guess my kids' health and well-being overrode my radical green impulses in that case," he explained sheepishly. To help us think about how context shapes who and what we prioritize, let's take a moment to discuss what are known as intrinsic and extrinsic values.[2]

Extrinsic values concern social standing and self-advancement. People with deeply held extrinsic values are likely to obsess over financial success, status, and fame. Intrinsic values, conversely, refer to aspects of life that we find inherently rewarding, such as those that concern relationships with friends and community. When individuals place greater importance on extrinsic values, they are more likely to express prejudice toward others, be less concerned about the environment, human rights, and animal welfare, and express lower levels of personal well-being and happiness.[3] Research looking at adolescents indicates a statistically significant relationship between strongly endorsed intrinsic values and an increased propensity to turn off lights in unused rooms, recycling, and a host of other pro-environmental behaviors.[4] Elsewhere we find indications of there being a strong positive correlation in adults between the size of their ecological footprints and their possession of extrinsic values.[5] You get one guess about which values are targeted by advertisers.

A group of researchers examined how watching Channel One, a daily ten-minute news bulletin with two minutes of advertisements, affected viewers' values.[6] Two neighboring schools with very similar student and parent demographics were chosen: one incorporated Channel One into its daily curriculum, the other did not. Teenagers enrolled at the school with Channel One reported much stronger attachment to extrinsic values than the control group. This corroborates other research finding meaningful links among hours of television viewing per day, a lack of concern for environmental problems, and an increased prevalence of extrinsic values.[7]

What is missed in all this talk about cultural values is that the medium is the message, to evoke an (often incorrectly applied) aphorism coined by Marshall McLuhan.[8] What I mean is that too often it is the *message* of advertising that is examined in this research—the content, the information conveyed. This leads to such questions as, Is the advertising encouraging status-seeking behavior or playing, and preying, upon body-image ideals, like the 2010 ad for pretzel sticks that read "You Can Never Be Too Thin"?

This brings us back to Joe, the executive from the previous section—specifically, to his point about the importance Big Food places on sentiments that travel well. We like to blame the messages used by Big Food to sell its wares, complaining that they distort the facts, play upon guilt, or feed outright ignorance. Yet limiting our critique to the message alone assumes we can actually say everything there is to know about food—remember, we know more than we can tell. But what if the medium itself was the problem? With foodscapes so stretched-out—spatially, socially, temporally—Big Food's only means to (cost-) effectively communicate with eaters lies with knowledge and sentiments that travel well. Multimillion-dollar celebrity ad campaigns: remember the milk mustache? Catchy jiggles: "Oh, I wish I were an Oscar Mayer wiener." Images of friendly faces: Uncle Ben, Betty Crocker. Pastoral images: the California Happy Cows campaign.

So many stories. Grocery stores are full of them, some autobiographical (country-of-origin labeling), others blatantly fantastical (Sponge-Bob SquarePants products). Alternative foodscapes tell stories, too. But theirs, as I'll detail momentarily, are premised on sentiments that tend to draw eaters *outward* in terms of what and whom they care about. When issues such as food worker pay, soil health, or animal welfare become more tangible, how do you think eaters will feel about Big Food?

Jill lives south of downtown Chicago. A single mother, she recently became active in neighborhood politics, which includes trying to alleviate the "food desert" problem in her community by encouraging urban gardens where abandoned buildings now stand and increasing the number of farmers' markets and farmers accepting Supplemental Nutrition Assistance Program (SNAP) benefits (formerly called "food stamps"). Now that her daughters are teenagers—which, according to Jill, means "they're too cool to have their mom around them 24/7"— she has time to pursue other things in life. Her family has also taken a growing interest in food—"*that* they're not too cool for," Jill told me. Where does food come from? Who has food, who doesn't, and why? "There's a lot that's hidden with the food that you buy at the store. It's not that everything is visible here," gesturing to the prepared food before us—eggs from her neighbor, bacon from the butcher down the street, and strawberries bought at a farmers' market. I couldn't actually see the farm these foods were raised on then and there in her dining room. But still, Jill admitted to seeing "a heck of a lot more" while acquiring those items than she might have seen had she tried "walking into Walmart."

She went on to highlight certain relationships, those encounters less amenable to stretched-out global supply chains, noting that even without setting foot on the farm, it is important to be able to talk with farmers. "How do they grow their food? Is it sustainable? How are their animals treated, for those that produce things like eggs? What's their mission statement?" From here, Jill pivoted to a point introduced earlier in my conversation with Joe, about how he was not paid to have eaters think too much, if at all, about things like livable wages for food employees when contemplating what to eat. Jill continued: "You might say that at places like farmers' markets you are not allowed to forget some of the very things Big Food would rather you not remember when thinking about what's for dinner."

I am not suggesting that a trip to the farmers' market will guarantee that shoppers will completely abandon industrial food. But what such places do seem to elicit is a greater sense of *ambivalence* about food—and that's significant.

The word *ambivalent* derives from the Latin prefix *ambi*, which means "both," and the Latin root *valentia*, which means "strength." Contrary to popular usage, ambivalence is not the same as indifference. When someone is ambivalent they possess feelings, attitudes, and beliefs that are in tension with each other. (The term was coined in 1911 by Eugen Beuler to describe the contradictory feelings that accompany schizophrenia.) To be ambivalent, then, is to possess, in sufficient amounts, both positive and negative feelings toward something. My interest in the concept lies in how we tend to respond to these tensions. When feelings are in conflict over a particular behavior, we tend to be more reflexive about it.[9] Bingo! That is not something those interviewed from the food industry want from their eaters, for them to be too torn over what they are eating. To quote Marcus, a senior marketing executive whose résumé reads like a *Who's Who* of major agrifood firms: "I want consumers to focus on just a handful of things when it's time to eat: a food's retail price, its taste, or other components where labels tell consumers all they need to know."

Ambivalence is not indicative of any particular behavior. Instead it has a mediating, and thus often moderating, effect. Studies examining attitudes toward eating meat, for instance, show that higher levels of ambivalence are correlated strongly with lower levels of meat consumption.[10] Another study explains how ambivalence shapes not only the quantity of meat that individuals consume but also can have a bearing on whether eaters are interested in the quality of life had by those animals prior to slaughter.[11]

Sarah lives in Chicago's west side, along with her two children. At one point in our interview the subject turned to the family's participation in a local farmers' market. Sarah had never (knowingly) met a farmer before shopping there. The same went for her kids. Sarah's work schedule—both of them, actually, as she works two jobs—can be hectic, which means the family does not always get to the market as often as they would like. During a particularly difficult stretch, when she was working extra shifts at one of her jobs, she hadn't gone to the farmers' market for a couple of weeks and had been doing all her shopping at a conventional grocery store. One particular trip stuck in her mind. Her seven-year-old asked an employee whether they had any free-range eggs. "'Do you have any idea how terrible battery cages are?'" she recalled her son telling the employee. "My jaw almost hit the floor. That would not have happened before we started going to the farmers' market." She continued, "We still eat conventional eggs if we have to. We're not hardcore about this. But we've learned from talking with people, you know, getting to know actual farmers, who don't use battery cages—it still makes me laugh that we know the lingo now. Conventional food doesn't want you to think about certain things, like about battery cages. I'm not saying knowing about them is going to change how you shop. But I bet it will make you think."

The lengths that "conventional food" goes to keep certain aspects of itself in the shadows cannot be overstated. Take, for example, so-called ag-gag legislation. In many states, these laws *criminalize* taking pictures, or videos, of the inside of an animal facility without the owner's consent. They must really *not* want eaters to know what's going on in those facilities. But such tactics only work as long as eaters are driven more by extrinsic than intrinsic values. The more we participate in the social life of food, the more we'll want to know about that life, and the less willing we'll be to buy from companies that refuse to show it to us.

Ethicists, dating back to Plato, have always presumed that *oughts*— those moral principles that guide behavior—precede *acts*. For millennia, we've been taught that morality is a top-down affair whereby we deduce what to value, formulate rules that reflect what we value, and then universally apply those rules to concrete situations.[12] That so few people actually lead purely ethical lives, following this model, has been taken by ethicists as evidence that modern life is somehow corrupting or immoral.[13] They rarely consider the alternative—that their own understanding of ethics is wrong, that rather than looking "up," we ought to be looking "down." If we accept that people are more than minds in vats—the brain-in-a-vat senario is a well-known thought experiment in philosophy, based on the assumption that all we know is held in (and who we are can be reduced to) the gray matter residing between our ears—then we must accept that *oughts* are not only about knowing, but also about feeling. In fact, that is precisely what makes them compelling. What happens when cold, hard logic leads to offensive outcomes? If objective reasoning produces an ethical principle that we find reprehensible, will we nevertheless adopt that moral posture simply on the basis of its rationality? Of course not. Moral principles need to feel right. And if they do not, if they go against what we know in our *gut* to be wrong, we discard them.[14] Notice how, even in our language about ethics, the body manages to sneak its way into the conservation.

Ethics, in a word, are made real through practice. "You can't *make* people feel differently about things; can't *make* them care; can't use reason, because people aren't reasonable, not in the traditional sense," said Bella, a teacher by training who left the formal school setting more than a decade ago. After leaving, she set out on a journey to, in her words, "engage in an experiment with experiential learning." She now owns a ten-acre farm that doubles as a classroom and a CSA. Community-supported agriculture (CSA), for those unfamiliar with the term, is a direct-marketing arrangement in which consumers pledge support to one or more local farms by paying upfront for a food subscription, thus sharing some of the risks alongside the farmer.

Struck by the comment that people are not reasonable in the traditional sense, I asked for clarification.

"There's just so much we don't understand about basic human behavior," Bella explained. "We think we have to appeal to some higher intellectual plane in order to get people to change their behaviors; reasoning with them that animals ought to have certain rights or that we have an ethical obligation to protect the Earth. When in fact, just the opposite is true. Give people the opportunity to experience food differently and I bet you'll get them to think and feel differently about things."

Bella's point, that thinking and feeling differently is born of *experience*, doesn't apply only to food. Anna Peterson writes about the 1954 US Supreme Court decision *Brown v. Board of Education of Topeka*, the landmark court ruling that struck down the infamous "separate but equal" rule for public education.[15] She notes how the ruling immediately changed behavior, which eventually led to new modes of thought and new ways of feeling—shifts that might have otherwise taken decades if left up to electoral politics. To quote Peterson at a particularly pivotal moment in her argument:

> Had the Court waited until most white southerners approved of integrated schools, my children might attend segregated schools today. As it stands, while school desegregation certainly did not end racism, it has had a significant effect on the lives and values of both white and black southerners. While southerners had to act as though black people were equal, even though most of them did not believe this in their hearts or minds in 1954, they were not acting morally, by Kantian or Lutheran standards. [...] Brown generated major shifts in values that probably would not have occurred had institutions and practices not changed first.[16]

Peterson goes on to suggest that "an environmental *Brown v. Board of Education* could help bring our practices into accord with our expressed values," with the added benefit, given how ethics tend to follow practice, of generating "environmental values as well as positive practical results."[17] I caution readers against immediately writing this suggestion off as an example of "nanny state" interventionism. Why? Because Big Food has already had its own versions of *Plessy v. Ferguson*.

Remember the aforementioned "ag-gag" laws. There are countless other examples. Baylen Linnekin's book *Biting the Hand That Feeds Us* provides a rich account of laws enacted under the guise of food safety that create significant barriers to entry for smaller-scale enterprises.[18] For instance, many ranchers and poultry farmers have to ship their animals hundreds of miles to be slaughtered and processed in a USDA-approved facility—a reasonable expense for large producers, who own their own fleet of semi-trucks, but a put-you-out-of-business expense for small producers looking to supply alternative markets. Or take the refrigeration requirements placed on vegetable growers. Regulations dictate the use of expensive mechanized refrigeration, even though less-expensive ice chests could perform the exact same job. Again, it's a perfectly reasonable expense if you produce many tons of produce annually. For those large-scale growers, it is likely even more cost-effective to use refrigeration rather than ice. Yet for the smaller-scale grower looking to fill a niche, the regulation is cost-prohibitive. And if you think ice chests can't be trusted to keep produce cold, food safety scientists are on record arguing they are actually *more* reliable than refrigerators. To quote one, "Coolers are cheap and reliable. Refrigerated trucks are expensive and susceptible to mechanical failure."[19]

These regulations blatantly favor the status quo while making it hard for alternatives to take root and prosper. Decades of such laws, government subsidies included, have shaped today's markets, not to mention our tastes and social environments. It's time for policy that nudges food in a different direction. I am not suggesting that alternative foodscapes do unto Big Food as Big Food has done unto them—that is, push for legislation that explicitly makes it hard for conventional producers to operate. But we cannot level the playing field simply by making food-safety laws scale-neutral and focusing on outcomes (e.g., everyone keep foods below 40 degrees Fahrenheit in order to retard bacterial growth) rather than processes (e.g., everyone use mechanized refrigeration). Shifting the power balance will require us to actively encourage alternatives such as making credit available to finance mobile slaughtering facilities, changing educational curricula to provide the next generation with opportunities to practice gardening and food preparation, and encouraging outside-the-box thinking like "double bucks," which double the value of SNAP benefits when people use them to buy local fruits and vegetables.

Such policy changes, to hearken back to Bella's point, would create opportunities for eaters to *experience* food differently, thereby leading them, eventually, to think and feel differently about what they eat.

Food literacy campaigns have yet to embrace a focus on experience. After all, common sense tells us that knowledge is the first step to change. Does this sound familiar? If only people knew what they're doing to themselves with their diet. How about this one: People wouldn't eat [insert demonized food here] if they understood how it's killing the environment. Or this: People just don't know how industrial food undermines livelihoods; if they did, they wouldn't eat it. This is where the never-ending drumbeat of "more education" comes into the picture. We just need to tell people why they ought to care about this stuff. Really? *Really?*

Let's begin with why these solutions are so attractive. They are largely apolitical. We don't really need to change anything, according to this approach, other than how we *talk* to each other about food.

The reality is a bit more complicated than that. This is not to say that we don't have reasons for doing what we do. We do. But it's naïve to think that, for instance, caring about the environment or knowing that fresh fruits and vegetables are healthy and ought to be eaten at every meal is enough to win legions of mouths over to alternative food movements. I do not know anyone who isn't already aware that fruits and vegetables are good for them, though you would never know it by looking at their diets. Rather than focusing on what we *think*, how we *feel* about food is far more predictive of behaviors, diets, and values.

How we *feel* about food: it's a difficult concept to pin down. It's related to attitude, though that term is too cognitive and disembodied. *Habit* might be a better synonym, as there is an important visceral component to what I mean by *feel.* Habit typically implies physically *doing* something, while leaving the door open to broader sociocultural factors that encourage a particular suite of *doings.* For instance, you might be in the habit of putting ketchup on your french fries, but don't delude yourself for a moment that this act is entirely of your own choosing.[20] *Why* do you put ketchup on your french fries—social norms? because you enjoy the taste of it? because you made it? because the ketchup lobby ensures that we're all exposed to this "vegetable" at an early age (according to the US federal regulations that oversee school meal plans, ketchup counts as a vegetable)? because it's fair-trade ketchup? because you don't like the taste of french fries without it (did you know there are substances in ketchup that block tastes by numbing receptors on your tongue, so drowning foods in this condiment *isn't* a compliment to the chef)? Answer these questions and you get closer to what I have in mind by evoking the term *feel.* It speaks to those visceral elements that drive our actions as well as those other (sociological) elements that turn one-and-done acts into full-blown habits.

The system that gives us global, everlasting food from nowhere pre-supposes an audience that feels a certain way about what it eats. This finding, that foodscapes live and die according to whether they can get consumers to feel them, is profoundly consequential and potentially revolutionary for those who can put it to work.

How do we do this? Well, it's complicated, in the sense that there are no one-size-fits-all solutions for the type of food revolutions I have been documenting. *No One Eats Alone* is a veritable buffet of examples of people coming together and experimenting, finding out what works for them. One area that we can't ignore, as discussed earlier, is government policy, though, as also discussed, it must be sensitive to the *hows* and *whys* (those aforementioned social elements) of food and not just the *whats* (e.g., *what* shouldn't be eaten, like turkey tails). After all, government is supposed to be the legal embodiment of society's collective values. But, given the state of our politics, is the state a savior or a bogeyman? Neither, actually.

The whole argument about whether there ought to be more or less government is as grounded in reality as my son's belief in Santa Claus. At least he'll grow out of this harmless childhood fantasy. In the adult world, you will often hear self-proclaimed champions of free enterprise argue for minimal government intervention in order to allow for the seamless integration of global markets. But this argument belies the reality of globalization. As Dani Rodrik, professor of international political economy at Harvard University, explains in a often-cited paper (provocatively titled "Why Do More Open Economies Have Bigger Governments?"), even after controlling for a host of variables, "there is a positive correlation between an economy's exposure to international trade and the size of its government."[21] International trade is incredibly risky. Governments must therefore grow in order to mitigate some of the risks that accompany it. In other words, without government intervention there could be no globalization or just about any market economy at all, for that matter—no contract enforcement, food-safety oversight, publicly funded roads and utilities, etc. That's right, the world envisioned by free marketers is, in fact, *dependent* upon government.

In the end, it is a matter of kind rather than of degree. *Who* does regulation help—the 1 or the 99 percent? Do we want government to support monocultures or polycultures? Do we want our government to create barriers to entry, by, for example, imposing costly, one-size-fits-all food-safety regulations and by enacting laws that veil eaters from the life of what they eat, such as through ag-gag legislation? Or do we want government to support competition, innovation, and experimentation, while empowering eaters to know more—not less—about their respective foodscapes?

Government isn't a panacea. But they—and lest we forget, government is made up of people, *eaters*—play a significant role in shaping our foodscapes. Let's make sure we include these eaters as we explore a new set of food values.

CHAPTER 4

Spatial Distance versus
Social Distance

This chapter takes aim at a sacred cow in alternative food movements: "local." If practices shape what we care about, then the potential of alternative food movements is not being fully realized by focusing narrowly on local food. After all, foodscapes can be "local," "close," and "compact" and still separate people.

"The old saying 'It's not *what* you know but *who* you know' is right but not for the reasons most think." Matilda, who lives along the Sunshine Coast about an hour's drive north of Brisbane, Australia, grows and sells flowers and vegetables at nearby farmers' markets and various local restaurants. She was telling me about how alternative foodscapes need to do more than provide people with access to affordable, wholesome, and sustainably raised foods, but also to make people feel differently about food—a discussion that eventually led to her describing what she called "food systems of care."

61

"We've lost touch with our food in Australia," she explained while scraping the dirt off a beetroot recently pulled from her garden. "I know I'm not saying anything that hasn't been said before, but there's something, something transformational and deeply meaningful, about having an actual relationship with the system that feeds you. How can you care about something you have no relationship with?"

The conversation later drifted to the issue of social justice—specifically, how to encourage eaters to care about not only the farmers but also all the other people who work to put food on our plates. "That's where we've got the most work to do," Matilda admitted. "We've done a respectable job getting people to think more about things like food miles and pesticides, even animal welfare, and you can't go anywhere without hearing about needing to put a farmer's face on food. Where we haven't done as well is with the other labor that feeds us, all that invisible work that comes after the farm. Farmers aren't the only ones that feed us, you know."

It's true. When talking to people who see themselves as part of the nebulous "alternative food movement," the subject of worker justice hardly comes up, not without my probing. Instead, I'm told repeatedly about the virtues of spatially compact foodscapes, of making food systems more local, with an eye toward reducing food miles. Often, though, social distance—living on different "sides of the tracks," so to speak—is a greater barrier than physical distance to people knowing, and thus empathizing with, each other.[1]

Big Food is perfectly content with this misdirection. As we've seen, food companies actively discourage eaters from thinking too much about matters like worker pay and pesticide poisonings. This is why I have repeatedly taken critics of the status quo to task whenever I hear them valorize spatial distance, as if *that's* the endgame—the creation of something like a bikeable foodscape. Here's the problem with that vision, or at least one problem among several: spatial distance can be co-opted by Big Food. Can and has. You need not look any further than Walmart's highly publicized foray into the local food market. Did this initiative bring eaters into closer contact with farmers, the land, farm laborers, or farm animals? For all their "progress" in reducing *spatial* distant between eaters and producers, Walmart's track record remains abysmal when it comes to reducing *social* distance. In fact, low wages of companies like Walmart cost American taxpayers roughly $154 *billion* a year through various public assistance programs because of Walmart's failure to pay a livable wage.[2]

Social distances have grown so great in countries like the United States that bringing people together for face-to-face encounters is becoming a real challenge. Forget about getting people around the same table to eat; even getting them to meet in the same room is harder than ever. We know, for example, that people with higher social status generally ignore those with less power. This phenomenon has been observed in numerous studies. Within a minute or two of meeting, the person with greater status begins to disengage from the conversation—less nodding and laughing—when paired with someone far "below" them on the social hierarchy.[3] They are also more likely to take over the conversation, interrupt, and look past the individual they are paired with, perhaps looking for someone more "worthy" of their time.

Part of this empathy gap appears to be due to wealth. The wealthy can hire help while those lacking material capital have to reinvest more in their social assets—the neighbor who watches one's child occasionally, the friend who is good with car repairs, or the woman down the street who is handy with a plumber's wrench.[4] Financial differences help produce behavioral differences, creating social distance at multiple levels—differences that go deep and shape how these groups feel about those around them.[5] This growing social distance, in all its various forms, can help explain the dynamics currently at play in Congress, from politicians' insistence on cutting financing for food stamps to their

rejection of universal health care coverage. Redistricting and gerryman-
dering have created virtual echo chambers, where elected officials have
less and less interaction with those different from themselves, which
means they also empathize less with them.

With all this social and political inertia pulling us apart, how do we
start to reverse course? It begins with what philosopher Charles Taylor
calls a politics of recognition.[6] We need spaces and activities that create
greater awareness among eaters (often white, often middle-class) toward
those socially distant "Others" (often nonwhite, often below middle-class) who have a hand in putting food on tables. This engagement
is too often missing from today's local-food projects, for one central
reason: it is a painfully difficult politics to enact. Yes, *painful*. Engaging
with people different from ourselves makes us uncomfortable.

Nora lives in Washington State, just north of Seattle. She described
her relationship with food as in "continual transition." Over the last five
years, she has started a small raised-bed garden, begun volunteering at
a local food bank, and joined a CSA. We had a memorable exchange
when the subject turned to her volunteer work at a local farm. During
one growing season, Nora, who identified herself as of European descent
and middle class, got to know a half dozen or so Han Chinese families
who also worked at the farm. They had an arrangement with the owner
that allowed them to work off their food bill. "We spent endless hours
shoulder to shoulder that summer, talking, laughing, eating together,
really getting to know one another," she explained. "It was such an eye
opening experience that I started bringing my kids. It really changed
how I think about food, and I think my kids would tell you the same
thing." Like many others I talked to, Nora admitted to "initially only

caring about the ecological footprint of food, or its nutritional profile." Ever since that summer, however, her understanding of food has "expanded."

"It really hit home the point that we need systems that are fair and just," she explained. "Too many players in the conventional system make ecological claims but still treat their workers like shit. I think you even see that among some claiming to be 'alternative.' That's not what alternative foods ought to be about. They ought to be about providing real alternatives, not just something slightly different."

We should not dismiss the value of spaces that encourage individuals from different backgrounds to get together, however awkward those encounters might be initially. As Nora explained to me, by talking, laughing, and eating with these otherwise socially distant families, she came to feel differently not only about them but also about food more generally.

For a non-food example, note how politicians cannot help abandoning their ideologies when their "gut" tells them to do so. And where do these feelings come from? *Relationships.* I am thinking specifically of Republicans who have been brave enough to break with their party on the issue of gay and lesbian rights and, more recently, same-sex marriage. All explained their change of position through the lens of social distance, or more accurately the lack thereof, as they all had someone close to them who had come out.

What I am suggesting is not entirely new. There is compelling evidence that the divisions in today's foodscapes discourage empathy, deterring people from caring more about various aspects of social well-being.[7] Food industry executives make precisely this point: that those separations are intentional because too much engagement could put them out of business—remember the ag-gag laws. Yet at what cost? We have all heard those distressing tales of eaters lacking basic food literacy. A recent study out of the United Kingdom, for instance, found that 36 percent of the 2,000 surveyed sixteen- to twenty-three-year-olds did not know that bacon comes from pigs, 40 percent failed to link milk with dairy cows (7 percent attributed it to wheat), and 33 percent were unaware of the origins of eggs (11 percent attributed eggs to wheat or corn).[8] The same study also discovered that three in ten of those surveyed born in the 1990s have not visited a farm in more than ten years. But even among those who do know these things, spatial and social distances help to normalize hurtful practices. As long as farm laborers remain invisible to wealthier consumers, employers will continue to treat them inhumanely.

Our failure to reduce the social distances that plague society means we shouldn't be surprised when eaters don't give a damn about certain key figures of the foodscape, like those toiling for little pay, sometimes under highly distressing—if not outright life-threatening—circumstances, so we can eat cheaply. Can we create foodscapes that result in eaters caring about others? Nora's experience is certainly encouraging. The following story is further cause for hope.

I have a keen interest in experiential learning environments, especially when those spaces pertain to food.[9] A couple of years back I was musing that people who think that immigrant laborers are stealing "our" jobs have never picked strawberries for a living. That stray thought led me to what I now refer to as the strawberry study. I recruited a dozen individuals from middle-class and higher economic backgrounds from northern Colorado. Household salaries of the sample population ranged from US$80,000 to US$175,000 a year. The group was an equal split between men and women, with an age range from twenty-five to fifty-six. In addition to their similar middle- and upper-middle-class backgrounds, they also shared a love for strawberries. And I readily admit to taking advantage of this trait when recruiting participants, by promising them all they could eat. Each individual was interviewed separately at the beginning of the study to assess their level of knowledge about the fruit. Questions like: How many do you eat a year? In season? And out of season? What do you know about how they are raised and harvested? And when is strawberry season in Colorado? California? Mexico?

Next, all participants were gathered together into a focus group, what one called a "strawberry palooza"—I had purchased a couple of ten-pound trays of the fruit for the event. Sitting around a table littered with strawberry tops and orphaned strawberry leaves, we watched a documentary about the industrial production of this fruit in California and then talked about what we saw. A week later we spent, as a group, seven hours picking strawberries at a farm. While doing this, participants were encouraged to use their phones to take pictures "of anything that so moved them." The study concluded a few days later, after backs and knees had time to recover. I met up with each for a debriefing in which we discussed their photos, their experiences picking strawberries, and how the project shaped their feelings about strawberries and food more generally.

One main goal of the study was to understand whether or not doing farm labor might alter participants' feelings about not only what they eat but also the very systems that put food on their tables. And I wanted to know how that hands-on experience compared with other methods of learning, such as watching a documentary or reading material about food. What I discovered from that initial one-on-one interview was that those involved in the study came into it knowing little about strawberries. Not one person could accurately state where strawberries from their neighborhood store came from at any given time of the year. Not surprisingly, then, none proved very good at guessing who did the picking. All twelve at some point made general references to "Mexicans," "Mexican Americans," and "Hispanics." The terms *illegals* and *aliens* were also used, once each. In other words, all at least understood that middle-class, unionized groups were not doing this work. Moreover, given some of the labels casually tossed about, you have probably already guessed that the participants were politically diverse.

The focus group offered what is known as representational knowledge. This is the stuff typically taught in schools, knowledge that can be *represented* through words (a textbook), graphs (X-Y scatterplots), and images (a map of the United States). It also travels well. This type of knowledge did appear to have an effect on participants, insofar as, after the focus group, they could, unlike when initially interviewed, name the top strawberry-producing locations in the United States and Mexico and describe some of the labor conditions in the harvesting process.

But while they could *talk* about the labor activities involved in industrial strawberry production, could they *feel* it? And how did that feeling, or lack thereof, translate into their behaviors as eaters? The act of picking strawberries, based on what was conveyed in final interviews, appeared a more effective means of making people feel differently about their food. And not just strawberries—respondents found these feelings generalizable to most fruits and vegetables that were picked by hand. Two participants even admitted to doing some research between the pick and our final interview to learn more about which foods are harvested manually.

The following quote is representative of the sentiments expressed in those final interviews: "The work was hard as hell, and we got to eat all the strawberries we wanted. I know if I were a field laborer I wouldn't do that [eat strawberries]. That would cut into what I brought home every day. So, even though I found that work unpleasant, it was probably a fraction of the unpleasantness that full-time field workers feel."

"What did you learn from your time out in the field picking?" I asked.

"A hell of a lot, actually. I don't know if I'd say I learned more than what I got from our earlier get-together [when the video was shown]. It was just a different type of knowledge, more meaningful in a lot of ways. You can't appreciate what those folks go through unless you've done a little of the work yourself. I've got to say, I'm more willing to pay a little more, shop locally if I have to, maybe even pick my own, now than I was before."

All twelve admitted to being moved by the picking experience. Three actually used that term—as in, to quote one of them, "I was really *moved* by that experience." It's a curious choice of words. We generally have a difficult time talking about things that are not easily representable. To convey such feelings, we tend to lean on metaphors—"I was moved by it," "it hit me like a punch in the gut," and so forth. As for the pictures, these provided another surprise. Initially, the images were overwhelmingly of people and landscapes: very generic, about nothing in particular other than to chronicle who was there and what the general experience looked like. But as the day progressed, so did the visceral feel of the photographs. By late afternoon, the photos took a noticeable turn: selfies of sweaty faces and wet, matted hair; one of a sweat ring in a baseball hat; a pair of soil-stained bare knees; and trays at various stages of fullness held by fingers caked with dirt and stained red. I do not think it was a coincidence that by the day's end everyone involved was taking photos documenting their physical exertion. For in the end it was precisely that—the "hard as hell" work—which stuck with them long after we left the field for our respective middle-class-and-above homes.

Recall my reference to the need for foodscapes that engender a politics of recognition. As the strawberry study demonstrates, one can no more get a feel for what it means to be a field laborer by being lectured about it than they can get a feel for riding a bike by reading instructions. Recognition has to be *experienced,* first-hand.

As you might have guessed, I am interested in how exposure to non-conventional food experiences affect people. It is tricky, however, to establish causality, as is always the case with anything involving social beings; unlike in laboratory conditions, we're never impacted by just one thing. What studies have been conducted on the subject look at the thoughts and actions of people *who are already enmeshed* in these activities.[10] Many of the stories recounted in *No One Eats Alone* are also of this sort. This is not meant to take anything away from those studies, my own included, that choose to examine eaters at a particular point in time. But it does call into question the issue of what caused what. Did the experience of an alternative foodscape lead to Feeling X . . . or did Feeling X, preceding the experience, draw the individual to participate? Correlation isn't causation. What we need are longitudinal studies: something, perhaps, where individuals are interviewed prior to "exposure"—to use crude experimental lingo—and then again well after having experienced a given set of practices, encounters, and routines. Only then would we be able to make more-forceful arguments about causation—about how, and perhaps even why, being embedded in a different foodscape changes the way eaters feel about food. If only someone could pull off such a study.

Well, it took some time—three years, to be exact—but I managed it. The complete findings of this research are reported elsewhere.[11] The bit I want to discuss here centers on evidence that these spaces helped instill within participants exactly that aforementioned recognition.

The research site: the Front Range of Colorado. I began by identifying eaters new to farmers' markets, CSAs, and food co-operatives. Not an easy feat, I admit. There were a lot of phone calls, e-mails, and, in the case of identifying new farmers' market participants, old-fashioned groundwork—pounding the pavement, pencils and surveys in hand, asking individuals if they're new to the space. Once identified, eaters were asked questions about their political and community engagement, how often they volunteer, their reasons for participating in these new foodscapes, and their levels of empathy for social-justice issues. Two years later, they were surveyed again and then interviewed in depth. A total of 119 eaters participated. Finally, a phone survey, which eventually yielded 106 responses, was conducted of randomly selected residents along the Front Range who did not belong to a CSA or a co-operative and who had not attended a farmers' market in the prior year. This population represented eaters who get their food from more conventional sources.

Most relevant to our discussion is what I learned about *why* eaters joined farmers' markets, CSAs, and co-ops. A number of studies report better taste and health as the principal reasons people choose these arrangements.[12] My findings support this research, with the following important caveat: these sentiments tend to hold *only for those new to these spaces.* Among conventional grocery-store shoppers, 79 percent listed "better tasting" and "healthier food" as the "most important" reasons for buying local and organic foods. Those participating in alternative foodscapes, when first interviewed, also ranked taste and health as being important—70 percent for CSA members and 63 percent for farmers' markets participants. (Those tied to co-operatives were most interested in supporting local growers and organizations. You'll need to read the peer-reviewed study to find out why.) When interviewed two years later, however, those rates dropped significantly, to levels below 50 percent.

One more clarification about methodology is needed before going any further. My CSA sample was actually two groups: (1) those exclusively involved in a drop-off CSA model, and (2) those participating in CSAs that offer a volunteer option. In the later model, eaters can work off some of their membership by planting, weeding, harvesting, etc. Those doing the volunteering tend to be a diverse group: people who volunteer out of financial necessity; well-to-do retirees; those wanting to learn more about where their food comes from. Given my story about the strawberry study, you can probably guess where I'm going with this.

For many participants, "exposure" led them to deemphasize taste and health as principal motivators and instead emphasize either "support for local growers and organizations" or "environmental sustainability." For example, among drop-off CSA participants, the "most important" ranking for "support for local growers and organizations" increased from 27 percent to 40 percent, while for "environmental sustainability," the ranking rose from 0 to 7 percent. Among those involved with farmers' markets, the "most important" ranking for "local growers" increased from 29 percent to 37 percent, while "environmental sustainability" increased from 9 percent to 17 percent.

Then we had the eaters working alongside others—volunteer CSA participants. While 70 percent reported taste and health as the "most important" reason for participating when first surveyed, only 8 percent gave the same answer two years later. Unlike drop-off CSA and farmers' market participants, which saw reporting shifts toward either "support for local growers and organizations" or "environmental sustainability," the volunteer CSA group reported a major reprioritizing toward "care for workers," rising from a response rate of 0 to 22 percent.

The problem with survey data is that it is sterile, even from a writing standpoint; it's hard to make prose lively when discussing percentages and changes in responses from Time 1 to Time 2. Quantitative data is devoid of stories, which is to say it is not a very good resource for delving into *why* people come to feel differently about things. This is where in-depth interviews come into the picture, allowing us to speak for data that can't speak for itself.

"Last summer I got to know someone from Nicaragua." I am talking here with Marti, who described herself as "upper-middle-class" and "white." In this exchange, she is telling me about how volunteering at a CSA led her to the seemingly mundane, but actually quite profound, "realization that food can either create divisions or create connections and togetherness." Back to her story about that individual from Nicaragua: "I went to learn about food and got a geography lesson instead. It was interesting; this fella was Native American. Not 'our' Native American. Native American to Nicaragua. I know, confusing. That's how he referred to himself: 'Native American.'"

She went on to tell me about how they began sharing recipes, one each week. This practice carried on for the remainder of the season, about five weeks. "I got interested in who this ethnic group was and started reading about them, in part so we'd have something to talk about." When she would take the recipes home, and try each dish, her children and husband started to participate in the lesson, too. "Most of the dishes were amazing—those I could get right, at least. We all learned a lot that summer, not just me but my entire household, about food, about Nicaragua and its indigenous people, about what it's like coming here as a brown-skinned immigrant." When asked why this mattered to her, in terms of making her more empathetic to others, particularly "Others" within foodscapes, her answer was surprisingly remorseful. "There's just so much space separating us, you know? Intellectually I knew that, we all knew that, before. But there's just something profoundly moving"— there's that metaphor again—"with experiencing, I mean, really doing it, not just reading about it in a book—different lives, cultures, and people. I regret not actively seeking out experiences that help tear those walls down. That's going to change."

Earlier I made passing reference to foodscapes that do more than put a farmer's face on food, as that particular agrarian ideal—that it's the farmer and the farmer alone producing what we eat—misses all the other labor that goes into keeping us fed: field labor; the valuable work performed by the natural environment and nonhuman animals; and all the service industry jobs we rarely think twice about—cooks, waiters, dish washers, and so forth. What this research documented was a measurable shift in how eaters thought about these "Others" as a result of being involved in the same (or at least similar) spaces they inhabit.

Changing our foodscapes is about more than rethinking what we eat. New spaces and experiences have the potential to fundamentally alter society as a whole, forcing us to reexamine the meaning of community, economy, and justice.

Distance: our approach to the concept is Euclidean—quantifiable space separating two points, conveyed in terms of miles, kilometers, inches, etc. But we can have very "near" foodscapes, or "short supply chains," in economic-speak, and still have participants who are effectively worlds away. My point is this: "local" is not enough to reduce the distances that plague our foodscapes. Here's to eating *with* others, in the deepest sense of the phrase.

CHAPTER 5

One Health

People around the world are hungry. They need food. And just as importantly, they need nutritious food: affordable fruits and vegetables, whole grains, lean proteins, and fast food. Wait, what was that last one?

There is a growing constituency of thoughtful, bright, and well-intentioned food scientists, public health professionals, and executives championing the health benefits of fast food. Seriously. This position made a particularly notable splash in 2013 when David Freedman published a piece in the *Atlantic Monthly* bombastically titled "How Junk Food Can End Obesity."[1] The essay extols the benefits of fast and cheap processed foods for improving the health of eaters around the world. I actually had the article waved in my face during an interview with an executive who oversaw the operations of a major firm's cereal division. Roughly ten minutes into the interview, with the magazine resting on her desk, she grabbed it, asking, "Did you see this article by Freedman?"

How could junk-food critics have been so daft? So many are shouting "Let's vote the bastards out!" when they really should be pushing for lifetime appointments. Ronald McDonald is dead, long live King Ronald!

It has been said that the twentieth-century bank robber Willie Sutton replied to the question about why he robs banks with the quip, "Because that's where the money is." In that vein, it does seem a bit disingenuous to criticize the development of healthier processed food options when that food is often the only thing available to food-insecure households. But there is also something dangerously shortsighted about pinning all of our hopes on items like the Charbroiled Atlantic Cod Fish Sandwich at Carl's Jr., which Freedman described as not only the "best meal" he had in Los Angeles but also "probably the healthiest."[2]

Wholesome, healthy, and *nourishing*: there is more going on with these terms than meets the eye. Realizing this reveals the superficiality of calls for greater nutritional literacy. At the risk of upsetting legions of dieticians and other health professionals, the current scope of most of these programs actually plays right into the hands of industry. Big Food wants eaters to hold fast to narrow understandings of "health," as that's the only way anyone could possibly grasp "eat at Carl's Jr." as healthful advice. Meanwhile, alternative foodscapes condition participants to feel differently about concepts like health. In many cases, this understanding is more in tune with the World Health Organization's (WHO) definition, which since 1948 has described health as "a state of complete physical, mental, and social well-being and not merely the absence of disease or infirmity."[3] Using this definition, an inexpensive, flavorsome, even nutritious 420-calorie fish sandwich can still be incredibly unhealthy.

"Did you see this article by Freedman?"

Okay, so the article wasn't *in* my face. But it was close enough that I could have reached and grabbed the magazine out of the executive's hand.

In fact, I had read the article, a couple of times. After telling her that, I decided to press her on the subject. Paraphrasing the WHO definition of health, I asked how she would respond to those who define health at a higher level, as being predicated on such things as how foods are raised, how well food workers are paid, and the sustainability of the practices used.

Elizabeth clearly did not expect me to parry her question with one of my own, and in *this* particular direction. Setting the magazine down she took about five seconds to assemble her response. "That's a *non sequitur*, as far as I'm concerned. I don't see the connection." She continued, "When consumers talk about health they're clearly interested in its ingredients and its nutritional context."

"I don't doubt that," I explained, "but I also know that health is understood differently depending on who you talk to."

"Well, then they don't know what they're talking about." Then, with her head shaking back and forth, she added, "That's not health. I admit food companies have an obligation to make sure consumers are informed about the nutritional qualities of their food. But our health and educational systems need to also step up, to make sure individuals know how to use that information, so they know what 'healthy' *really* means."

No one else was quite this direct, essentially taking a my-way-or-the-highway stance on the subject of health. But while Elizabeth's stance might not match others in terms of tenor, it paralleled that of her peers in other ways. When the subject of health was brought up among those affiliated with industry, all—*all*—took this to mean that I wanted to talk with them about the specific makeup of their foods. In the words of one food scientist, in response to being queried about the health claims in recent advertisements about a product she was responsible for concocting, "I can talk about the chemical makeup of our food all day. What do you want to know?"

Why this highly reductionist understanding of health? *What* is to be gained, and by *whom*, by grasping health so narrowly? Talking to the

Maori in Aotearoa (the Maori name for New Zealand), I learned that they reject Western reductionism, favoring a far more holistic interpretation. For them, good health is a balance among mental (*hinengaro*), physical (*tinana*), family/social (*whänau*), and spiritual (*wairua*) dimensions.[4] This echoes what I was told by the Native Americans I spoke with, as well as every person interviewed with connections to the worldwide peasant and small-scale farmers' movement, *La Vía Campesina*.[5] Yet these groups were not the only ones to espouse holistic attitudes toward health. A surprising number of eaters—low-, middle-, and upper-income—in affluent countries, especially those exposed to food-based experiences that reduce social distance, spoke of knowing health in ways that Elizabeth and many of her peers wouldn't approve of.

Processed breakfast cereal starts life as a big undifferentiated mess of goop. Cereal manufacturers learned decades ago that by mixing grains with water—what is called, unappetizingly, grain slurry—and putting them through a machine called an extruder they can turn undifferentiated raw inputs like corn and rice into gold. The extruder forces the grain slurry out through a tiny hole at high temperature and pressure. The shape of the hole determines the slurry's ultimate hardened state, such as little o's (Cheerios), big colorful O's (Fruit Loops), hexagon-shaped discs punctuated with little o's (Honeycomb), shreds (Shredded Wheat), or puffs (Corn Pops). From the extruder, cereal is then shuttled over to a nozzle and sprayed with a coating of oil and sugar to postpone the inevitable sogginess that follows contact with milk. Extrusion also, however, strips grains of their nutrients. So cereal needs to be fortified: a process that, not coincidently, allows for still further product differentiation and gives firms an opening to charge consumers a little more for their product. As I learned through my interviews, a couple of cents' worth of fortification allows manufacturers to charge anywhere between twenty-five to fifty cents more per box at retail, a rate of return that would make even Bernie Madoff envious.

Industrial foods are often fortified because they need to be. Micronutrients have a hard time withstanding the scorched-earth-like environments that are food-manufacturing floors. Manufacturers therefore turn to industrial vitamins and minerals to make their wares "healthy." It's not just cereal—though I dare you to find a cereal box that doesn't make multiple health claims. The ubiquitous health signage on most processed foods proves this point: Big Food loves Big Vitamin.

Back up. What's this about *industrial* vitamins and minerals?

"I was responsible for making food healthy. More than just fortifying food, I was helping fortify the entire industry." This quote comes from Yuk Wah, a retired chemist who previously worked for a Chinese company in charge of supplying most of the world's vitamin D.

Here is a fun game: count the number of times in a day you eat something derived from Australian sheep. It is actually not much of a game at all, as just about *everything* that goes into the average Western eater's month contains something from Aussie sheep. That something is vitamin D. Approximately all the world's manufactured vitamin D, which is in just about everything these days, comes from chemical factories in China where most of the world's manufactured vitamins now originate. The raw input used to make it is lanolin, from sheep imported from Australia.[6]

The irony was not lost on Yuk Wah. "I always found it a bit comical," he confessed.

When I asked why, Yuk Wah's answer was remarkable for its forthrightness. "We're talking about an industrial processes, the processes involved in manufacturing these vitamins." By this point he was smiling—he really did find it comical. "I mean, that's what it is—an industrial process. The industrial effluent, the smell, and the emissions—it's ironic, really. We're in a business that's supposed to make our food and by extension people healthier. But our practices—let's not forget we're talking about China, where regulations are especially weak—these practices are endangering public health." He then paused. Listening to the recording, I got the sense he was weighing just how much he should say. I am forever grateful for what he decided to share: "We're trying to improve individual health at the expense of public health. Maybe *ironic* isn't the right word." His smile at this point had disappeared. In its place was a look that resembled, perhaps, contrition. He then added, "It's sad. Sad that that's what's going on and sad because we've gotten to a point where public health and individual health have come to mean different things."

Yuk Wah is right. It *ought* to make us sad. Just look at the food-energy footprint for the average American eater. After factoring in production, processing, transportation, and retail, the final daily per capita tally is more than 17,000 calories.[7] (Again, this is not how many food calories are available to each individual but how much energy these sectors collectively consume on a daily basis in order to feed the average US citizen.) Breaking those energy units down according to specific food categories, we find that over half go into the making and distribution of highly processed foods, a third into animal products, with the remaining sixth going toward grains, fruits, and vegetables. What industry insiders like Elizabeth and well-intentioned food writers like David Freedman miss in their praise of processed food is the point that *processed* is a euphemism for "energy subtracted" and "greenhouse gases emitted." But that's just the tip of the cost iceberg when we rely on fast food and industrial nutrients to solve our diet problems.

"That's a tension all governments face, not just the US." Ted has been with the United States Department of Agriculture (USDA) for over twenty years, working in the area of food safety and inspection before moving to the Food and Nutrition Service division. There, Ted and others, along with members of the Department of Health and Human Services (DHHS), live and breathe dietary guidelines, especially every fifth year when the guidelines are revised. "Look at our role here. We're tasked with increasing food production and protecting public health." He is referring to USDA's unambiguous charge to support US agriculture, perhaps most infamously through farm subsidies, while at the same time improving American diets, through the aforementioned guidelines. The math, however, of this "produce more + protect public health" directive does not always add up. Ted explained: "Even if we weren't talking about food, that's a questionable mandate. But it *is* food we're talking about. And even healthy food, when eaten in excess, isn't good for you. We're caught between a rock and a soft spot"—a phrase he had used earlier in the conversation to refer to the farm lobby (rock) and obesity (soft spot).

I then asked about the steps being taken at the federal level to resolve the tension between producing and selling (which usually means *eating*) more and eating healthily.

"Industry generally supports the trend toward having the nutritional information on all food items. They see the writing on the wall. It's going to happen and they've discovered it might actually work in their favor, something they can make money from by being able to charge more for something." In case you missed it, Ted just affirmed my point that the heuristic "health = nutrition" equation not only protects the status quo, but also turns health into a commodity that can be sold, often at a premium. He continued, "It has been a delicate balancing act, between public health and massaging the messaging about how much of a given food or food group people should be eating. They do not like it when consumers are told to eat their foods in moderation, for example. And we all know what happened when we attempted to broaden the discussion to issues of sustainability."

Ted is referring to a draft recommendation circulated by a joint USDA/DHHS advisory committee in December 2014. The group had the audacity to think outside the individualized health box by suggesting that nutritional guidelines be tied to some broader notion of sustainability. It certainly makes sense to me: the premise that healthy foodscapes ought to be able to feed current and future generations without spoiling the environment in the process. Admittedly, the document drew its conclusions with a brush broader than the one I would have used. But it was only an early draft. The one stroke that really raised the ire of industry noted that "a dietary pattern that is higher in plant-based foods, such as vegetables, fruits, whole grains, legumes, nuts, and seeds, and lower in animal-based foods is more health-promoting and is associated with lesser environmental impact (GHG emissions and energy, land, and water use) than is the current average U.S. diet."[8] *How* those plant-based foods are produced—and the degree to which they are processed—matters enormously from the standpoint of sustainability.[9] But, again, it was an early draft.

Before the report was even issued, the US House of Representatives passed a bill directing the agriculture secretary, Tom Vilsack, to focus only on "sound nutrition science and not pursue an environmental agenda." Industry has also aggressively, through lobbyists and endless statements issued by its own experts, sought to keep the environment out of eaters' understanding of health. It looks like they will get their way.

My conversation with Ted eventually circled back to his remark about how listing the nutritional content of foods might actually work in industry's favor. "Business is all about creating environments that enhance your competitiveness," he added. "Food companies with market share and an army of chemists will thrive in this new world where everyone's suddenly health-conscious. But that success hinges on consumers reducing health to the numbers on a food's Nutrition Facts label. It's like that juice we were talking about." His voice then slightly changed, as if he were imitating someone. "'Oh, it has vitamin C, let's give it to our kids at every meal!'" And then in his original voice: "It's just bona fide sugar water, no better than soda."

We had discussed juice earlier in the interview, in particular the expansion of imports from China into the US market. China aggressively expanded its apple production in the late 1990s. Not long thereafter, Chinese apple producers soon found themselves with mountains of apples—those too small, too misshapen, too off-color, and in some cases even too rotten to sell in the "fresh" market.[10] So they followed the lead of US turkey producers (chapter 1), though rather than creating markets for turkey tails, they developed supply chains to extract, package, and distribute juice made from these discards. But wait, people don't drink apple juice in China. No problem, they do in the US; nearly 60 percent of all apple juice in the United States comes from China. When Chinese apple juice concentrate entered the US market, its price dropped from US$153 per ton in 1995 to US$55 per ton in 1998.[11] For once, the United States was on the receiving end of dumping, involving a food group that many nutritionists would place in the same "eat sparingly" category as the fatty turkey tail. As Ted alludes to above, apple juice is essentially the nutritional equivalent of Coca-Cola, with the added branding bonus of potentially being labeled "all natural" and even "fresh" in some instances.

It just so happens that I interviewed an individual who had a hand in "juicing the United States," as he called it. Mark has been exporting juice from Asia to North American markets since the mid-1990s. His comments perfectly parallel Ted's. "Orange juice, a mainstay at the breakfast table for generations, has taken a hit recently. But overall, juice consumption has remained steady in recent years." Mark's right. Sales of orange juice have dropped almost every year since the dawn of the new millennium.[12] At the height of the market, almost three-quarters of American households had O.J. in either their fridge or freezer.[13] "Sure, it's not a fixture at breakfast tables anymore, but it's making inroads elsewhere—all those healthy juices you see at Starbucks and at grocery stores," he added. "Even most soda vending machines sell them, though now the move is toward 100 percent juice, fortified varieties."

Right again. According to beverage industry reports, approximately half of US consumers who purchase "100 percent juices" look for no-sugar-added varieties, and 40 percent want vitamin- or nutrient-enhanced formulations.[14] No dummy about consumer treads, a few years back Coca-Cola launched a new line of orange juices under the brand name Minute Maid Pure Squeezed. The line is available in four varieties: No Pulp, 100 percent Orange Juice; No Pulp, 100 percent Orange Juice with Calcium and Vitamin D (a.k.a. essence of sheep); Some Pulp, 100 percent Orange Juice; and Light Orange Juice Beverage with Calcium and Vitamin D. Or note Starbucks' move into what is called the "super-premium juice segment" of the market with its acquisition of Evolution Fresh Inc. and its "never heated" juice products, a pasteurization technique said to keep nutrients intact during the juicing process.

"But 100 percent juice is still 100 percent calories from sugar," I pointed out to Mark. "And you know better than anybody that there's nothing healthy about the juice market in China." I am referring to the China Huiyuan Juice Group, headquartered in Beijing, which is the largest privately owned juice producer in the country and controls more than 60 percent of China's 100-percent-juice market. That level of concentration is decidedly harmful.[15] Pausing to smile, signaling that what was coming should be taken as provocative rather than insulting, I asked, "So why call your juice 'healthy'?"

"Point taken, mate, but that's not going to work for me."

Earlier I had asked, "Why this highly reductionist understanding of health?"

Mark gave me an answer: "I'm not going to be able to sell product if we all started thinking like that."

Sue and Ricky live north of Seattle in the lush Skagit Valley. A few years back, they began supplying pork to a chain of local restaurants. It almost did not happen. The restaurant's owner initially only wanted the succulent shoulder, one of the animal's juiciest cuts.

"When we first started talking, that's all they were interested in buying from us," Sue told me. "It was like getting punched in the gut. When we learned they wanted to buy from us we thought: This is it—something really exciting is about to happen! Then we had that first phone call, 'We only want pork shoulders.' Okay, so I turned to Ricky and asked, 'What do they expect us to do with the other 80 percent of the animal?'"

Ricky and Sue eventually convinced the restaurant owner to buy their ham as well and mix the two: four parts ham, six parts shoulder. Together, the shoulder and ham constitute between 40 and 50 percent of the animal's total carcass weight. "We could work with those numbers," Ricky explained. "It's not hard to find buyers of our loins and bellies [bacon]. Plenty of higher-end restaurants to take those. That just leaves various miscellaneous parts that we ground into sausage."

Sitting around their kitchen table we talked about the difficulties faced by farmers when trying to grow and sell to local and regional markets. With the smell of coffee and deviled eggs in the air—an admittedly strange pairing, but the eggs were their own and they were delicious—we discussed this whole-animal problem. It was at this point that my hosts began offering more biting critiques. Ricky was especially unforgiving when describing what health means to what he called "conventional food supporters," versus how it's understood by people like himself and Sue, who refuse to divorce it from animal welfare and the well-being of natural and human communities.

"The industrial system has gotten to the point where chickens are damn near nothing but two giant breasts." He said this while reaching for a framed picture of himself standing in a pasture among chickens and cattle. Handing the picture to me, he continued, "Our animals have to do more than just make white meat, so they can't be just breasts on legs. For one thing, our animals have to actually walk so they can clean up after our cattle and hogs while fertilizing pasture behind them." After pausing a few seconds to let me look at the picture, he added, "People don't fully appreciate the difficulties we face trying to hook up a polyculture to a system not designed for diversity. The whole-animal problem is a symptom of a larger pathology."

A symptom of a larger pathology: strong words. Yet for those trying to cultivate polycultures, and live cultures, too (we mustn't forget about microbes) such phrasing is strikingly apt. Take the case of non-therapeutic antibiotic use in livestock agriculture. Big Pharma allows Big Food to practice the highly concentrated hoof-to-hoof (or beak-to-beak) model of animal confinement that gives us cheap meat. Antibiotics given to livestock make up more than 65 percent of the global total, with the rest going for human use. In the United States, that breakdown is even more skewed: 80 percent of antibiotics are used for livestock and 20 percent for humans. Globally, the use of antibiotics for animals is expected to rise. Currently, about 64,000 tons are consumed yearly by the livestock sector worldwide, a figure expected to exceed 100,000 tons by 2030.[16] In the United States, according to the US Food and Drug Administration, sales of antibiotics sold to farmers and ranchers for use in animals grew by 16 percent from 2009 to 2012.[17]

Antibiotics are used on livestock farms for four reasons: (1) treatment of disease; (2) metaphylactics, by which the presence of clinical illness in one animal triggers treatment of the whole herd or flock; (3) prophylactics—in other words, a preventive measure; and (4) growth promotion, which represents the most common reason of the four.[18]

Since the 1950s, producers have been adding low doses of antibiotics to animal feed, which causes weight gain of up to 20 percent. The underlying mechanism remains poorly understood, though one theory is that calories normally allocated to fighting routine intestinal and digestive infections are instead directed to building fat and muscle. Antibiotics allow animal crowding to occur, as they reduce the likelihood of disease when animals are packed together, while allowing the industry to reap the economies of scale that come with this practice. But it's a slippery slope, as the incentive to overcrowd is great, and antibiotics are cheap. And so, further crowding intensifies the "need" for still more antibiotics, which begets still more crowding, and so on.

Ricky again: "That's a healthy animal for a lot of vets [veterinarians] today, an animal juiced up on antibiotics and hormones. Heck, a healthy animal seems to be anything that hasn't succumbed to its miserable existence. How did we get to this point?"

This is not leading up to one of those holier-than-thou "if they only knew better" claims. Individuals who use these drugs are not bad people—they are simply responding to socioeconomic factors. My work has brought me into contact with dozens of people working in conventional foodscapes who are concerned deeply with animal health, from veterinarians based in the United States, China, and New Zealand to animal scientists from six universities in five countries and managers of feedlots in the United States and Brazil. On this point they all agree: antibiotics are required for "health." Read this not as an endorsement of pharmaceuticals, but as an indication of the sad reality about the welfare of a feedlot animal. If you want to get rid of antibiotics on the farm, you have to create an environment where they are no longer "needed." It is as simple, and as difficult, as that.

A concrete example will help make my point: organic dairies. Proponents of the status quo are fond of pointing to this industry, with its higher culling and disease rates, when making the case for non-therapeutic uses of antibiotics. These higher rates, as I am often told, are the result of farmers being unable to treat sick cows with antibiotics. But is that really a fair comparison, between industrial non-organic dairies and industrial organic dairies? It is a bit like saying that the only way to reduce car fatalities is by making cars larger, noting how people who drive smaller models do not fare as well in accidents, while never bothering to consider that the fundamental "problem" is not car size but automobile transportation itself. If we had not organized our cities in a way that requires us to drive, we would not need tank-sized vehicles to stay safe—we would not need cars at all! Similarly, if our foodscapes did not create conditions that make animals sick, we would not need nearly as many antibiotics. (Norway and Denmark are able to use a fraction of the antibiotics used in the United States on a per-animal basis, because they have radically altered animal agriculture.) Less-intensive organic dairies employ very different nutritional and management strategies compared with large, intensive operations. Organic restrictions on the use of pesticides and herbicides in the production of animal feed tend to encourage organic dairies to employ grazing to an extent not seen in more industrial settings, especially among smaller farms where rotational grazing makes sense. More grazing equals less-intensive feeding, less confinement, and, ultimately, animals that do not "need" antibiotics.[19] As for animal health under these alternative regimes: cows in less-industrial, organic dairies live 1.5 to 2 years longer than their confined cousins.[20]

Voilà! Foodscapes populated with healthy animals—no antibiotics required. Which means healthier foodscapes, too, lest we forget about a not-so-little thing called antibiotic resistance.

Food distance is often considered in narrowly Euclidian ways—that is, in the strictly geometric, spatial manner discussed in the previous chapter. We tend to see health in a similar way, separating the "inside" (usually pure, clean) and "outside" (where disease lurks), as opposed to understanding disease as a *relationship*.[21] The former is about border-*lines*—when did building walls become a solution to so many of our ills?—the latter, about border*lands*.[22] In walling out "bad" life, conventional foodscapes are harming other lives, such as *ours*. Bacteria are not the only lives lost in this preemptive antibiotic war. Lest we forget, we ourselves are mostly bacteria—in cellular terms, at least. There are ten times more bacteria cells in our bodies than human cells.[23] We all know of our mammalian and even reptilian ancestry—consider, for instance, the reptilian (triune) brain. Yet an ancestry rooted in bacteria? Looks like it. About forty of our genes appear to be bacterial in origin.[24] No wonder some microbiologists are suggesting that we rethink the category of human, reimagining ourselves as a "superorganism" of inter-related metabolic processes that include microbes.[25] (Gut microbiota, for instance, have recently been linked to brain activity and emotional behavior in humans.[26]) Thanks to dominant agricultural practices, we have managed to summarily boot many of these companions from our lives, changing *us* in the process.

If we consider these relationships, it becomes clear that overuse of antibiotics is endangering our lives and those of future generations by hastening antimicrobial resistance. To help myself understand this process, I talked to a science advisor for the World Health Organization, Joyce Markus. She confirmed how the view of health that pits a clean, pure, and safe "inside" against a contaminated "outside" overlooks the complexity of disease, especially in confined-animal-feeding operations

(CAFO). "Resistant bacteria that develop in CAFOs are being trans-
ferred to the general human population through food." Did you catch
that? The danger lies *within* CAFOs, due to the ecologies of these spaces,
not outside of them. "Government officials and medical health professionals are becoming seriously concerned over food-borne diseases, like
those caused by Campylobacter and Salmonella bacteria." According to
the Centers for Disease Control and Prevention, there are roughly 50
million cases—about one in six Americans—of food-borne illness a year
in the United States, 3,000 of which are fatal.[27]

Joyce again: "We carry Campylobacter right into our homes, our
kitchens. Most of the poultry we buy is harboring it, and if you don't
thoroughly cook the meat you are going to get sick—maybe not deathly
ill, thank God, but sick nevertheless." Up to 250 of the 2–4 million
Campylobacter infections per year result in deaths in the United States.[28]
About one in a thousand Campylobacter infections also leads to Guil-
lain-Barré Syndrome, an affliction that can cause paralysis.[29] In short,
drug-resistant Campylobacter is a real public health concern.

The poultry industry's use of fluoroquinolones, a class of broad-spec-
trum antibiotic, has led to the development of resistant Campylobacter
strains. Prior to the approval of fluoroquinolone in US agriculture, the
only cases of resistance reported were in people who had either taken the
drugs for therapeutic use or traveled to a country that permitted their
use. After its approval, resistant strains began emerging in samples taken
not only from poultry but also from humans who had never taken the
drug or traveled overseas. Evidence of resistance was so great that the
FDA banned fluoroquinolones from veterinary use in September 2005.
Their use in agricultural applications is still allowed in other countries,
however. Equally worrisome is the increasing number of resistant Campylobacter isolates that have developed resistance to other antimicro-
bials, such as macrolides, aminoglycosides, and beta-lactams, many of
which are still allowed in US animal livestock operations.[30]

To be clear, I am not suggesting that we abandon antibiotics, which can be life-saving drugs. What I *am* suggesting is that we approach health in the same spirit as we approach other subjects discussed in this book. To speak of needing a *healthy* appreciation for relationships and complexity is more than rhetorical flourish. Rather than making assumptions that unwittingly cast the world, and *us* with it, as black-versus-white (like "bugs-versus-humans"), we would do well to think about health in more collaborative terms.

A while back I received an e-mail from a colleague, an epidemiologist from the Boston area. The subject line of her message read, "Turns out education and exercise INCREASE your risk of heart attacks." More than a little intrigued, I opened the attached document and found an article from the journal *Circulation* by Andrew Odegaard and colleagues at the University of Minnesota School of Public Health. The article tells of people flocking to Western-style fast-food chains in Singapore and reviews the results of these dietary changes. Curiously, those making these culinary "choices" were younger and better educated, exercise-conscious, and nonsmokers, all factors that ought to be associated with lower risk of heart disease. Instead, this demographic was demonstrably less healthy than other populations who might exercise less, smoke more, and were less educated, all because the latter group avoided American-style fast food. Singaporeans eating fast food once a week had a 20 percent higher likelihood of dying from coronary heart disease than those whose lips never touched the stuff. That rate increased to 50 percent for those eating fast food two or three times a week, and to almost 80 percent among those who ate fast food four or more times a week.[31]

Not that Singapore is special in this particular respect. Just look at what is afoot in the United States, where we find ourselves staring down an unenviable precipice. Hundreds of counties, most located in southern states, have seen their average life expectancy decline in recent years; these are counties that, not coincidently, also have some of the highest obesity rates in the nation, in addition to very high levels of inequality.[32]

Conservative estimates calculate that 30 percent of the increase in health care spending over the past twenty years in the United States can be attributed to the rising rate of obesity. Others place that figure at closer to 50 percent, noting that the condition now accounts for 21 percent of total national health care spending.[33] It is no wonder that a national conversation has been taking place around the subject of health care reform. Yet as Michael Pollan asked in a *New York Times* op-ed piece back in 2009, "Where is talk about food reform?"[34] While there is little agreement over what it ought to look like, everyone in the United States thinks health care reform is necessary, even after—or especially after, in the eyes of some—passage of the Affordable Care Act, popularly known as Obamacare.

But what good is individualized health care reform if we leave the social body malnourished and diseased? Can you have real reform without addressing the underlying factors that cause illness and malcontent? Of course not. And yet, throughout much of the world, you see government policies that, with one hand, subsidize practices that make "us," in the broadest sense, sick, while the other is busying treating these self-inflicted wounds in the form of government-supported health care.

Additional answers are required before decreeing that the Charbroiled Atlantic Cod Fish Sandwich at Carl's Jr. is "healthy." What about, for instance, the issue of labor? Were field laborers used in the harvesting of the sandwich's lettuce? Were they paid fairly? The indentured servitude-type relationships that exist in the fresh-produce trade, so we can eat "healthily," is one of the many sad ironies I learned about while researching this book.[35]

Those in alternative foodscapes *are* asking these questions, perhaps not always loudly, perhaps not always with answers, but at least they are challenging convention. Don't take my word for it. To quote Julian, a community activist living in Denver:

> The more I'm involved in these regional food initiatives, the more I'm convinced that food and agricultural policy are inseparable from community development and public health initiatives. I'm interested in growing healthy communities. I really don't give a shit about how much vitamin C or dietary fiber a food has. If it's destroying communities, it's unhealthy. End of story.

The healthy solution, then, isn't some-*thing*, which thus precludes us from buying, and Big Food from profiting massively from the sale of, "it." Meat (grass-fed vs. grain-fed, hormone-filled vs. hormone-free, etc.); so-called alternative protein sources (e.g., crickets, legumes, tofu); packaged processed foods fortified with vitamin D from China; eggs from local farmers' markets: what makes these foods healthy, or not, lies in the lives they affect. In the end, those interviewed, like Julian, were interested in making health a political matter—remembering, of course, that health is, already-always-and-forever, politics by another means. By challenging how we think about and practice health, alternative food-scapes help make "it" no longer about just what the Nutrition Facts say. Instead, health becomes something much broader: health is about who—humans and nonhuman animals; microbes too, at least the sym-biotic ones—are being afforded space to live well.

CHAPTER 6
From Slow Food to Connectivity

Walking up their driveway, I passed a 1990 Volkswagen. Nothing out of the ordinary about it, except for the two bumper stickers displayed on its rear window: one read, "Slow Food"; the other, "If I'm Speeding It's Because I Have to Poop." Chuckling, I reconciled the mixed messages, thinking the car was a hand-me-down, from parent to child. I knew that the owners, whom I was about to interview, had two teenage sons. (I was once a teenage boy myself. Enough said.) I did not think any more about those stickers until weeks later, while reading through the transcript of my interview from that day. I never asked if the messages were intentionally placed side by side, perhaps even by the parents.

"My colonic transit time is thirteen hours." Steve lives in Vancouver, Canada, with Julie, his wife, and their two teenage sons. Steve and Julie are very active in local food politics, from serving on or advising numerous food-policy councils to working with school administrators from around the region to get more locally grown foods into their cafeterias. He continued, "For the average male, it takes about thirty-three hours for food to go in the large intestine and come out as poop. That is what you get with fast food: slow bowels." This comment alone made my interview with Steve and Julie unforgettable. That was before I was shown an x-ray of Steve's large intestine. And yes, he did point out to me his fast-moving poo.

I will be returning to my interview with Steve and Julie later this chapter. I mention it here, bumper stickers and all, to highlight this simple fact: when we talk about food in relationship to pace, nothing is black and white. "We need to practice food more slowly!" Sounds sensible, especially given the glorification of *fast*—fast food, fast line speeds, fast-maturing beef cows, and fast-growing salmon. But that is precisely the type of fight Big Food wants. Why? Because pace is contextual. By focusing on pace, what is to stop any of us from slowing down *here* only to speed up *there*? That is what McDonald's "You Deserve a Break Today" campaign was selling: respite from an otherwise hectic life—a type of slow food, some within industry would argue. Besides, as Steve's colon reminds us, what's so great about slow anyway? *Slow* is far from aspirational, for example, if it's the result of feeling sluggish. Or worse: constipation.

"They're looking to cater to neo-gastronomes, people who are interested in good food, gastronomic pleasure, and who wish to enjoy their food at a slower pace." I was sitting in The Corner in Sydney, Australia, near the University of Sydney, talking with Hugh, a consultant who specializes in masking corporate food in hipster guises. The setting of this meeting was intentional. No golden arches were anywhere to be seen. The only sign that I was sitting in a McDonald's-owned restaurant was the "McCafé" in small cursive print below the restaurant logo. We were discussing why firms come knocking on Hugh's door. Hugh continued by explaining how his "clients are trying to have it both ways." In his words, "Sometimes it pays if you're Pepsi to yell it from the mountain tops; other times a more subdued posture is necessary when trying to win over millennials looking for something new."

Individuals like Hugh are becoming the toast of the party within food-industry circles as Big Food searches for ways to slow down and offer eaters greater authenticity. Like PepsiCo's Caleb's Kola soda: it comes in a glass bottle and is sweetened with cane sugar and "kola nut extract"—whatever *that* is. There are no signs that the drink is from the same manufacturer who gives us such iconic brands as Pepsi, Mountain Dew, and Gatorade. Instead, bottles prominently bear the phrase "Honor in Craft." Talking to people like Hugh made it clear what Big Food is trying to do with these ventures into hipsterdom. They're selling slowness.

The slow-food movement itself is partly to blame here. (The movement was founded in 1986 and today has well over 100,000 members in 150 countries.) As its own website admits, it "began with an initial aim to defend good food, gastronomic pleasure, and a slower pace of life." It was only later that the movement "broadened its sights to embrace issues such as the quality of life and the health of the planet that we live on."[1] If the initial aims of the movement sound familiar, that is because you just read most of them, in Hugh's opening quote. He took artistic license, noting that his customers wish "to enjoy their *food* at a slower pace." Food companies that seek out Hugh's services aren't interested in people enjoying a slower pace of *life*, because then they might have time to eat elsewhere. Like at home.

"The aim of a place like this"—Hugh raised his hands as if giving a prize away on a game show—"is to give people a memorable, relaxed, pleasurable eating experience. It's 'Slow food for the rest of us,' I like to say."

"Slow food for the rest of us?" I asked, trying not to sound incredulous.

His answer told me a lot about how Big Food wants eaters to grasp slowness: "Slow food is about pleasure, right? We're just interested in making an affordable eating experience that's pleasurable for customers."

He makes a good point. It is almost impossible to read about slow food without being told of the importance of pleasure. Carlo Petrini, the founder of the movement, devotes an entire section (titled "Pleasure Denied, Pleasure Rediscovered") to the topic in his book *Slow Food: The Case for Taste*.[2] The problem with the term *pleasure*, however, is that it is laden with both positive and negative connotations. Petrini rightly repositions the term, noting that when used in the context of slow food it is not meant to be synonymous with excess or decadence—many of the world's religions scorn certain types of pleasure, like those linked to physicality.[3] Yet even with that repositioning, the term still suffers from a significant problem, which is precisely why it is being co-opted by Hugh and his clients. It pulls individuals inward.

"My clients have been telling people to slow down for ages. Take McDonald's and their 'You Deserve a Break Today' slogan." That campaign, I later learned, dates back to 1970, and was only abandoned in 2014—the very year, coincidently, that the company started experimenting with The Corner. "I'm not saying anything that people don't already know," Hugh explained. "The average person is under tremendous pressure. They need to get the kids to and from school, get to work on time, meet deadlines, maybe even work weekends. I've never agreed with the label 'fast food.' It's just the opposite, in my mind. It's food that allows people to slow down, even if just for fifteen minutes."

But here's the catch. Using Hugh's definition, "slow food" arguably supports, and perhaps even speeds up, the hectic pace of modern life. It does nothing, for example, to change largely invisible but deeply felt norms that act as high-octane propellants in our daily routines. We live in a world full of social expectations, demands, and pressures that maintain the mode of capitalist food production. Hugh and his clients certainly do not want you to forget all those things that we "need" to do:

sticking to deadlines and schedules; working evenings and weekends if we wish to remain employed; working evenings and weekends so we can afford that medical procedure or those looming college tuition bills; and then there's that trip to Hawaii we think we need. Hugh even mentioned some of these pressures, apparently to make sure that I didn't forget them, either. The very system claiming to promote freedom certainly doesn't allow us much when *freedom* is framed in these terms—a bit like saying you're free to work like a dog or to live like one by choosing to be unemployed and without health care.[4] Note that Hugh says nothing about wanting to slow the system down. He's just interested in slowing down the individual, and just the individual during those fifteen minutes when they are in his client's establishment. There is nothing radical or threatening about that. And this is the point. The slowness Hugh and other insiders actively promote does not really change anything.

The following is a description of the slow-food delicacy cappon magro: "The dish consists of layers of mixed seafood, salsa verde, potato, and smoked tuna. With all the boning, shelling, cleaning, and chopping, it takes three people five hours to make a real cappon magro. It is worth every minute, though."[5] *Three* people working *five* hours to make a *single* dish? Who, especially among the working class, has time for that? And if it were made, who within the household would most likely be responsible for its preparation?

I have been speaking in gender-neutral terms up to this point. But food is not, nor has it ever been, gender-neutral.[6] Who are most likely to possess those aforementioned skills that play such an important role in diversifying our foodscapes? Who then will be expected to transfer them to others in the community as we grow these alternative food futures? The answer for each question is the same: women. When food writers—sorry, Michael Pollan—are asked to give eaters advice and respond by saying, "Just cook!," I cringe.[7] Intellectually, it may sound like solid instruction. But that is also its problem; it is a recommendation abstracted from the realities of lived experience, especially among populations (read: women) that already struggle under the weight of time poverty. My interviews support existing research on the subject. Specifically, women in these alternative food networks (like their peers in industrial foodscapes) generally face greater time pressures due to role expectations that place them at the center of it all—harvesting, canning, pickling, freezing, cooking. . . . And let us also not forget that all this is often *on top* of other household "duties" like cleaning, errand running, and child care.[8]

It does not have to be this way. Fortunately, we can look to real-world examples of people working together to ensure that their alternatives make time for those populations most strapped for it.

Melissa is a single mother with three children, all between the ages of seven and eleven. She also resides within a United States Department of Agriculture (USDA)–defined food desert in Chicago's Lower West Side.[9] She works twenty hours a week cleaning rooms for a major hotel chain and another ten hours, over the weekends, cleaning for two local businesses. "I just don't have time to cook, not like I'd like," she explained to me. "Never really taught to begin with. My mom was like me—too busy to sleep, let alone teach her daughters how to cook." Later in the conversation, as we talked about community-led food projects, she added, "I think it's great. Most people are like me. Too busy. Before, I didn't even know you weren't supposed to eat the seeds of [green/red] peppers. This is allowing my oldest and me to pick up some cooking skills while the other two play with other kiddos from the neighborhood."

Melissa is referring to a series of community cooking workshops that offer child care while also allowing interested children, like Melissa's oldest, to participate in the "class" if they wish. In order to diversify the skills taught, as not everyone in the community wishes to eat "white"—such as the European-style dishes I ate while growing up in rural Iowa—the workshops draw on the culinary miscellany of the neighborhood.[10] "This is all community-led," I was told by one of the organizers responsible for making this program happen. He continued, "Members of the community propose workshop 'topics'"—making air quotes—"as we're a diverse people. And members of the community, who possess the culinary expertise, teach others." A little later in the conversation attention turned to the issue of how many in the community are time-poor. "It's a great way to share knowledge and broaden people's taste experiences while being sensitive to time constraints," he told me. "Hell, on more than one occasion I've even taken my car to pick people up, if transportation is somehow a barrier for them."

Catherine tells a similar story. Her husband drives long-haul trucks across the country, often leaving her alone with their four children—all younger than the age of sixteen—for a week at a time. Catherine works at home and admits to "wanting to do more to provide locally produced, fresh, homemade food" for her family. "If I only had more time," she told me. "I don't have enough; the days aren't long enough to even get the basics covered. Sometimes I confess to feeling like it's a bit of a luxury, thinking I can provide my family with more foods from my kitchen."

Recently, Catherine's neighborhood in Philadelphia, Pennsylvania, started a program directed at families precisely like hers, those that may be "time-poor but rich in enthusiasm," as she describes her situation. This program offers a space where residents can acquire new skills—in this case pickling and canning. Child care is provided as well as transportation in the form of someone's minivan making prearranged stops throughout the neighborhood. But more than just skills, the program also gives participants access to space, equipment, and even food to do their preserving. The food, much of it surplus from local growers that would likely otherwise go to waste, is either donated or sold to organizers for a nominal fee. Participants then pay what they can for their enrollment in the program.

"I love it," Catherine told me as she walked to her fridge. Opening it up and pointing to a jar of pickles, she said proudly, "I made those. To be able to go someplace where I can take my kids and have the vegetables already there. I don't have to go to the store or a farmers' market and lug back thirty pounds of cucumbers. Do you know what a time-saver that is for someone like me? To have access to a pressure cooker and the jars and everything. For me, it's not about the money. It's all about the time."

Making time. It is a principle that lies at the heart of the slow food movement, or so its most ardent supporters have told me. And yet, *how* we go about doing this matters immensely. Melissa and Catherine are part of communities that reject the whack-a-mole approach to slow food—slowing down *here* only to speed up *there*. Instead, they are investing social and cultural capital to make time for those who lack it. Others I interviewed, including numerous apostles of slow food, confessed that the only way they could slow down in the kitchen was by rushing through other activities. How is that transformative?

This point was eloquently, if begrudgingly, made by Arlene, an active member of the Denver chapter of Slow Food, the organization founded by Carlo Petrini in 1986. "We need to make time to grow connections," she explained. "Those connections have been lost—with our food, with our community, even with our families in a lot of instances. That's what slow food is about: connections and taking time to make them."

I certainly agree about the importance of connections, but it's still not clear to me how the movement makes time so people can get together. So I asked how Slow Food tackles those structural realities and norms—those expectations that say you "need" this and that.

After a few false starts—I clearly pushed the conversation into a gray area she wasn't expecting—Arlene found her footing, though her voice lacked its previous brightness. "I'll admit, this is all easier said than done. Not everyone has the time to do these things. That's something we need to work more on. Slow food needs to be something everyone can do. I'll admit, at the moment it's not."

Perhaps. Or maybe we need to regroup and revisit our terms. But if not *slow*, then what?

Rather than couching this discussion in terms of either fast or slow, allow me to suggest an alternative, namely, *mobility*. Concepts related to speed—like slow—tend to refer to the movement of a body through space. They speak to phenomena that are measurable and quantifiable. The food executives I interviewed calculate time spent in the kitchen, grocery store, or restaurant down to the minute, sometimes even to the second. To quote one, "Consumers today have insanely busy lives. A lot of them are looking for meals that can be popped in the microwave for sixty seconds."

In another interview, a thirty-year marketing veteran with extensive experience working with fast-food chains had this to say: "The average American, employed full-time, spends less than two hours a day with their kids. That's what we're selling: time—time for people to spend more time with child and elder care, or whatever else is important to them. Some of the products I've helped market will get you in and out of the kitchen in less than thirty minutes. Others, like my work with [a major international fast-food chain], offer the option of not having to set foot in the kitchen at all. It's fast food but with the aim of giving people a break. Who can argue with that?"

Then there was my interview with a designer whose specialty is the in-store built environment. This individual consults with chains on things like seating arrangements, interior decor, kitchen design, plate size, and even things like what seasonings ought to be available on every table. "Generally, a family spends a fixed amount of time at an eating establishment—what I call in-out time. That time might vary from family to family; each household has their own time. Let's say a family's in-out time for a particular sit-down restaurant is seventy-five minutes. That tends not to change regardless of whether they get their food within fifteen minutes of sitting down or forty-five minutes. However, the quicker they get their food, within reason, the better they rate their eating experience. So I always try to find ways to get food to patrons more quickly so they can take their time and enjoy themselves."

I interviewed researchers who, with multiple stopwatches in hand, not only time how long shoppers spend in grocery stores but also plot their paths and measure precisely the amount of time spent in the various departments. They then try to figure out why consumers lingered in Department X while rushing through Department Y. I also met with fast-food executives who obsessed over things like the frying time of their french fries and how long it would take their cashiers to enter each customer's order into the register. And I had coffee with a major vegetable grower who told me how quickly he is able to turn a field of lettuce into endless crates of bagged salad. *Quantitative* time, perhaps not surprisingly, was remarkably important to those embedded in more-conventional foodscapes. As the old saying goes, Time is money.

This is not to suggest that measurable time is unimportant to those experimenting with alternatives. As the prior section made clear, everyone wants more time, and rightly so. When rushed, it seems impossible to do more—particularly to cook, can, tend a garden, save seeds, or eat together as a family. But some eaters are concerned with more than time. Rather than focusing myopically on pace per se—How long does someone have to do X?—many alternative foodscapes are engaging questions of mobility. Who? Who moves fastest, farthest, most often? How? How do we move and how comfortable is it? What? What routes are being taken? And Why? Why does a person or thing move and why does it stop?[11]

To consider the politics of mobility, take the examples of farmers' markets that are intentionally located on the border between socially and economically divergent neighborhoods. The city walls of yesteryear have been replaced by less visible dividers: public transportation systems that bypass entire "bad" neighborhoods; grocery stores (and even many farmers' markets) that do not stock ingredients needed to make certain "ethnic" dishes; restaurant and grocery chains that steer clear of certain parts of a city. All these dividers, each in its own way, create friction (to use a mobility-related metaphor), which shapes who goes where and why and how those experiences are felt.[12] I interviewed more than a dozen people of color from lower-income households who described having to travel to often white, always more-affluent neighboring communities whenever they need to buy things like local fruits and vegetables and meat. To quote one individual: "If I didn't need to do it I wouldn't. I just feel out of place whenever I go there. Not that it's easy to get there. I've got to change buses three times." Then with a smirk she added, "You'd almost think they didn't want people from my neighborhood coming there."

Compare that statement with the following, from an individual who lives in a non-European, lower-income neighborhood in Sydney, Australia. Yet in this case, the fresh food markets are concentrated at a point where numerous neighborhoods converge. "Those markets don't belong to any one neighborhood. They belong to all of us. It's an incredibly welcoming environment."

A number of the growers, local politicians, and urban food activists whom I talked with noted the importance of *connectivity*. Some even suggested that we abandon our obsession with distance and speed, and designations like "local" or "slow." In the words of an individual who served on one of Auckland, New Zealand's, twenty-one local boards, "Distance and speed play into the hands of corporate food and ignore what really matters for those of us interested in creating just food systems, as if that is something that can be reduced to a number. Food from so many kilometers away, or that has been in transport for only so many hours, or that comes with an advert telling you how busy you are—that's not the stuff we're interesting in. Does it encourage sociability? Are the retail spaces made so all stakeholders feel welcome? Are we making sure we're bringing neighborhoods and people together? Those are the questions I want answered. For me, it's about connectivity."

He brought both hands up just below his chin, made two fists, and held them together. "Think of these hands like communities or regions, even households. They're close, touching in fact. But they're not connected." Grinding his firsts together, he noted: "When you try to connect them it just doesn't feel right. It's hurts, actually." He then opened his hands and interlinked his fingers: "Slow food, fast food, local food: none of that really matters anymore when you have systems designed with an eye toward connectivity. Foodscapes that make people feel welcome; that take into consideration stakeholder needs. Those things matter a lot more than whether the people are eating a meal in fifteen minutes or two hours."

I conclude this chapter where it began, with my encounter with Julie and Steve and their speedy colons. "The point that people need to remember," Julie explained, "is that the fast/slow dichotomy is more a strategy for entering into a deeper conversation about food's role in human flourishing."

I asked her how we should then talk about food, if not in terms of speed.

"I'm not saying anything new but I think *care* is a better word." She continued, "That's what this is all about: encouraging people to care more about their food and the people involved in preparing it." This concept certainly aligns with efforts to make foodscapes more welcoming—that connectivity piece. Massimo Montanari, a professor of medieval history at Bologna University and well-known food-studies scholar, made exactly this point about care some twenty years ago. It is worth quoting the source, as both Julie and Steve acknowledged having read this specific piece, originally published in a 1996 issue of the magazine *Slow*.

In my opinion, it is just a matter of care: Caring for the selection of ingredients and the resulting taste, caring for food methods . . . caring for the sensory messages conveyed by what we eat, for presentation, for the choice of people sharing the food with us, etc. An endless series of caring for which, in my opinion, can be applied to any circumstance with equal dignity: a meal at home or at the restaurant, a drink at the pub or a sandwich in a snack bar. . . . When assessing the quality of these experiences, what makes the difference is not how long they last: it all depends on whether we are willing and have the possibility of experiencing these events with care. This requires a structurally "slow" culture, the capacity to understand and assess, a critical disposition which may—or may not—be there at any one moment.[13]

There is a lot to unpack here—plenty that is tantalizing, too, like his talk of a "structurally 'slow' culture." I certainly think that Montanari's point about care is important, though it is unfortunate that the subtlety he shows by rejecting the fast/slow dichotomy is later abandoned with his claim "our foe is not 'fast food,' but 'careless food,' the culture of careless food."[14] As shown in prior chapters, Big Food is not care-less but care-differently. I think that what Professor Montanari is trying to say is that foodscapes need to engender more capacity for critical reflection. How we help develop that is to some degree the very subject of this book, though for me, *reflection* implies something felt as much as thought. Reflection can suggest an act that draws eaters inward. The spaces described above place a premium on activities that encourage "we" over "me" thinking and feeling. The solutions encouraged, then, are aimed at social bodies, and thus the *creation* of more time, rather than just individualized bodies, where the only thing created is the *perception* of more time.

CHAPTER 7

Buying Behaviors versus Building Community

"Legislation is one thing; behavioral change is something else entirely." This obsevation came from Nicole, a nutritionist employed by the USDA within its Food and Nutrition Service agency. We were discussing the challenge of getting school-age kids to eat differently. A few years back, the federal government introduced a new rule requiring schools to serve an extra $5.4 million worth of fruits and vegetables in lunchrooms across all fifty states daily. Nicole described this particular piece of legislation as "eye-opening," for it made her realize that "offering healthier options and having kids actually eat healthy are two completely different challenges." She added, only half-jokingly: "What that legislation really amounted to is it increased fruit and vegetable waste in our schools by some $5.4 million daily." US schools are actually wasting $3.8 million of that $5.8 million daily investment, according to one study.[1] Regardless of the actual figure, there is a lot of food being wasted in our schools—even more now, thanks to those new federal school-meal rules, which arose out of the 2010 Healthy, Hunger-Free Kids Act.

As opposed to most elected officials in Washington, federal agency employees—who get and keep their jobs through hard work, not by saying and doing bombastic things—are, generally speaking, a thoughtful lot. I knew, therefore, that Nicole and others at the USDA would not take this waste lying down. So I asked about next steps: "What's the plan for changing habits, for getting more of those fruits and vegetables eaten?"

After spending a few minutes telling me about the need for "greater nutritional literacy among kids as well as their parents"—I never said that agency employees are infallible—Nicole turned to the subject of incentives, explaining how "we're starting to pay greater attention to incentives and rewards." Perhaps assuming she was talking to an incentive skeptic (correct!), she added, "I initially pooh-poohed the idea, paying kids to adopt behaviors they *should* be doing just feels off—am I right? Yet the initial research on the subject led me to change my tune to the idea. Incentives seem to work."

There is an old saying in the social sciences: be careful what you are looking for because you will probably find it. The adage is a reminder to be reflective about the questions we ask and the assumptions we make in our quest to answer them. Nicole is right. Incentives do work. Therein rests the problem, recognizing that the most dangerous untruths are truths slightly distorted.[2] Incentives have shown themselves effective at creating *short-term* behavioral changes. But then what? What happens next, after an incentive has elicited the desired behavioral change? And what happens when that incentive disappears? No one thinks these rewards ought to be doled out forever.

The research Nicole mentioned was a study involving fifteen different schools that measured the effect of small rewards on behaviors in the lunchroom. The researchers varied the incentives given across the schools: some kids got a nickel for eating their fruits and vegetables; other children received a quarter; and still others were given a raffle ticket for a larger prize. The results of these weeklong experiments were generally the same, regardless of the award.[3] These relatively small, inexpensive rewards increased fruit and vegetable consumption by 80 percent, thus reducing the amount wasted by 33 percent.

Problem solved? Remember what I said in the introductory chapter, about how real change can only be had by changing the social milieu of foodscapes? Incentives do nothing about this. Instead, they risk creating greater social isolation and apathy among eaters, pulling us in the very direction we need our foodscapes to pull us *away* from.

"I'll cut right to the chase." Geoff is a Hong Kong–based marketing executive who oversees food-related advertising campaigns throughout much of Southeast Asia and Australasia. He started out teaching economics and business management classes to undergraduates at a university in Australia before putting, as he explained it, his "background in behavioral economics to work in the business world." He went on to tell me about how "economic incentives alone rarely work if the aim is to create lasting behavioral changes. Apparently that's news to some, because government and public health officials are enamored with the idea, a case of knowing just enough economics to be dangerous."

The incentive road is a slippery one. The more people are externally rewarded for socially and environmentally positive actions, the less likely they are to be driven by internal motivations. This is also known among economists as the "crowding-out effect": intrinsic motivations are crowded out by external rewards.[4] Some of the earliest research on this effect dates back to the early 1970s. Looking at various blood donation programs, researchers observed that those paying people small amounts to donate their blood actually had lower donation rates. The researchers reasoned that this practice broke established social norms about voluntary contribution.[5] In other words, attaching a monetary price to the practice caused some potential volunteers to no longer view the transaction as selfless but selfish. Another now-classic study looked at high school students collecting donations for a charity in a door-to-door fund-raising campaign. Students invested more effort when they were not compensated than when a small payment was offered.[6] Even in instances where incentives are sufficiently attractive to change behaviors, those changes are almost always temporary. The moment the external monetary reward is removed, practices typically resort back to what they were pre-incentive. We are therefore left with the following rather unflattering conclusion about the practice: incentives risk creating short-term behavioral changes at the cost of producing people who have an eroded sense of social responsibility toward others and the environment.

Geoff continued: "It's disappointing, really, that some of the loudest advocates for changing the food system approach the subject with a hammer when what they need is not only every tool in their toolkit but access to the tool factory itself—hell, to the entire tool market."

Smirking, Geoff paused to let the comment sink in. Clearly he wanted me to ask. So I did: "Every tool in the toolkit? Access to the tool factory? The tool market? I don't get it."

"The success of industrial food," he said, "lies less in getting any one tactic right than in having their hands in multiple subtle cues, which collectively are immensely powerful." With that, Geoff launched into telling me about priming and modeling. Take priming. "We know that the type of music playing in a store or restaurant's background can influence purchasing decisions. My company did some research on that very subject about a year ago. Consumers are remarkably susceptible to environmental cues." While I'm not familiar with Geoff's internal research—he was not willing to share any of those documents with me—there is plenty published on the subject. One study, for instance, randomized whether costumers were exposed to French or German music in a grocery store and then monitored wine purchases. When French music was played, French wine outsold German wine by a ratio of three to one, yet when German music was played, German wine outsold French vintages.[7]

The concept of priming might make it appear as though consumers are fickle, even irrational—or at worst, as easily manipulated dolts. But that could not be further from the truth. It just means that humans are, well, human. Priming is part of the very human (and nonhuman, in some cases) tendency to look for signals from our environment—heuristics or scripts, as they're often called—when making decisions. This can be especially true when dealing with phenomena outside our sphere of experience, like French and German wine for the weekend oenophile. Priming also allows us to speak to the more sinister side of incentives. The simple *presence* of money can affect our behavior, and not in a good way. Research has shown that mere exposure to the concept can have socially deleterious effects, such as by reducing altruism and increasing social distance. In one study, participants were primed by the presence of a large pile of Monopoly money. Those exposed to this play money were less willing to help someone who had "accidentally" spilled a box of pencils. In another scenario, participants were asked to fill out questionnaires while seated in front of a computer monitor with a screensaver that depicted either money floating or fish swimming. Exposure to the floating cash reduced participants' willingness to work in a team and resulted in their seeing themselves as having less in common with the other participants.[8]

Let's go back now to the idea of paying children to eat their vegetables. Are we willing to trade generosity for better nutrition, assuming that the incentives work in the short term? I don't know. But it's a question worth asking. Regardless, it's reason enough to be cautious about such approaches. The whole point of the incentives was to get kids to see dollar signs at the salad bar. How can we expect to build healthy communities when we're actively encouraging a love of money at the expense of collaboration?

Marisa works for a major marketing firm in London. A social psychologist by training, she spent a good deal of our interview describing the need for a robust "social architecture," which she described as "that stuff that allows us to approach those nudging instruments like incentives as if they were training wheels, where after a while you can take them off without worrying about the whole thing crashing." When asked what she meant by "social architecture," she offered an elegant first principle: "We tend to eat like those we trust."

Diffusion is a social process through which people talking to one another spread an innovation, explains Everett Rogers, who spent roughly half a century studying how new ideas, technologies, and techniques are communicated and dispersed.[9] Mass media can be effective at introducing a new idea to people. But, as decades of this "diffusion literature" have shown (we're talking about a research tradition dating back to the 1930s), people tend to follow the lead of those they trust when deciding whether to do anything with new knowledge. I tell my students to think about this in the context of electoral politics: political ads might alert you to a candidate's record, but how you vote is ultimately based on conversations with others whom you know and respect. The field of "influencer marketing" is solidly rooted in this research. Influencer marketing? I will let Marisa explain.

Getting an endorsement from a trusted third party is a million times better than anything you or your marketing department can come up with. When talking about food, that could be a popular

blogger or someone with a large Twitter following. So I might rec-
ommend finding popular bloggers that fit your brand or who write
about your industry and send them free stuff and hope they like
your product. Maybe even offer to give discounts or freebees to
their readers, anything to hook a positive endorsement, and then
maybe promise them a percent of sales they drive your way.[10]

She went on to explain her sympathy for those looking to "take
us"—industrial food, I presume—"down." "Look at the head start we
have. And resources, flying bloggers in to trade shows, giving them
the royal treatment so they'll not only 'like' us"—a Facebook reference—"but take the time to tell their followers why they should be
buying our stuff rather than getting it from our competitors. That's
an expensive endeavor, my friend." She's right—it *is* expensive. It is an
expense that most in the alternative food movement could not afford
if they wanted to. She is wrong, however, to say that it is the best way
to influence behavior.

Regional foodscapes, it could be argued, are the originators of influencer marketing, as many interactions at this scale are repeat encounters, which build not only trust but also empathy, compassion, and
feelings of care for the others—"Others"—that feed us. In many ways,
alternative food networks are better positioned in this game of trust
than industrial ones. "I don't believe people really trust food bloggers,"
said Lana. "You follow a food blogger who has a lot of followers, but we
mistake that following for trust when in fact it's just people using rules
of thumb to make decisions, rules like 'A lot of people are following
Blogger X so I should, too'." Lana lives in Atlanta, Georgia. She calls

herself a regional food entrepreneur, a title more fitting than the one on her business card, which rather blandly reads "Community Planner." As Lana explained, her passion is "building connections between farmers, consumers, and those third places where people get together to eat, like restaurants, cafes, food trucks, pretty much wherever food is eaten outside the home."

Lana's story is interesting. She has, in her own words, "come back from the other side," noting that "in a prior life" she worked for a couple of major food companies in their marketing departments. "Back then, Facebook was really popular, so we'd rate food writers by their number of 'friends.' The more friends, the higher value they had in our eyes. This is where we need to be careful throwing around a term like *trust*. Facebook friends are a poor measure of it. People are more apt to follow someone with a huge Twitter following, or a large bank of Facebook friends, for the same reason they go see a movie that's breaking box-office records. We assume all those 'hits' tell us something about the quality of the thing we're interested in, but they don't. That's what we do as humans, look for shortcuts to make sense of a world that's noisy and complex." (Remember my point earlier about heuristics or scripts.) She concluded this line of thought on an optimistic note, explaining, "These trends to model behavior we think are normal are quickly cancelled out in the face of alternative behaviors from a trusted source. That's our ace in the hole. The alternative food movement is a movement of trust, first and foremost, or at least it ought to be—bridge building, community building. By building relationships there isn't anything food companies can do to override those sentiments. I'll take social relationships over a flashy celebrity ad campaign any day."

That has been my point all along. The only way to change long-term behavior is to build community.

Jeff is a self-proclaimed community organizer and small-scale farmer whose property is roughly a thirty-minute drive north of Minneapolis,

Minnesota. "The success of the alternative food movement," he said, "lies in people realizing this is more than just about food, about people choosing carrots and locally grown eggs over Pop-Tarts and Mountain Dew. This is really a movement about creating community." More than once he told me, "I'm trying to grow healthy communities."

"Why frame it that way, through the lens of community?" I asked, already knowing the answer to this question—it's my job as a sociologist to know—but wanting to hear how he was connecting the dots.

"Anything less is tinkering around the edges," he responded immediately. Sitting straight up, his hands clenched on the table, Jeff added, "People don't like to talk about a 'food revolution.' I'm not even sure that's the right word, as it assumes the options are black and white, but it captures the scope of what we need, of something profound, something deep."

Jeff is right, on both counts. We need a revolution, but not in the sense of some epic contest between a thickly muscled juggernaut—Global Capitalism, Neoliberalism, Big Food—and a spry and yet fledgling Resistance. We cannot simply replace one status quo with another. And as for his comment about needing a change that reaches "deep," again I couldn't agree more.

For all the attention paid to incentives, the surer bet lies with the social structures described by Jeff, Lana, and dozens of others with whom I have spoken. I am talking about those networks that not only influence what's available and at what price but also how foods are perceived and by whom, and the relationships that make foodscapes desirable and doable, in terms of making sure they make available time, skills, and so forth.

For behaviors to stick, they need to be repeated. (This is why I am not terribly impressed with schemes like agri-tourism. These one-off encounters may raise awareness in a shallow sense, but they don't tend to change long-term behavior.[11]) There is a grossly ignored element of the adoption-and-diffusion model that goes a long way toward explaining why people choose to adopt the behaviors, techniques, and technologies they do. Unbeknownst to Everett Rogers, the model he spent most of life studying, right up until his death in 2004, makes some pretty important distinctions between explicit and tacit knowledge—that is, knowledge we can tell and that which is more than we can tell.

Recall that this research strongly supports the conclusion that while mass media is effective at introducing new ideas to people, it is noticeably less successful at getting people to change their minds and alter their behaviors. For that, according to Rogers and colleagues, you need people to talk with each other, and if they trust each other, so much the better. Here is where Rogers stumbles. In overselling the power of talking, he misses what else happens when people get together over something new, whether a food, a recipe, a seed, or a farming technique.

As I have mentioned repeatedly, one of the major barriers to alternative foodscapes is a deficit in tacit knowledge: not knowing how to cook, or how to select foods from farmers' markets (or from one's own garden), or how to grow or save seeds. Paying consumers to eat their vegetables or subsidizing polycultures is not going to miraculously wipe away this deficit. This kind of knowledge requires practice, practice, practice.

No doubt, interpersonal communication helps. When encountering something new, whether a farming technique or a novel vegetable, we inevitably talk about it. We ask questions—for instance, "What the hell am I going to do with all that chard!" But these exchanges involve more than just information. While long understood as a theory of communication, the adoption-and-diffusion framework implies a physical component. According to this literature, trial and observation increase the likelihood of adoption. Bingo! Adoption has as much to do with *working with* alternatives as it does talking about them—perhaps even more, in some cases. In sum: you have to get people physically engaged with alternatives to make them stick.

Habits created through incentives rarely stick, because we lack the social infrastructure to keep them in place once the reward is removed. This explains why, for example, farmers put their land back into conventional production when conservation-reserve programs expire. (Even when engaged in the desired behavior—keeping the land out of production, planting native grass varieties, etc.—"most of us," to quote one producer, "are guilty of doing a pretty half-assed job. We're only doing it to get paid. What do you expect?") For the same reason, we should not be surprised when kids go back to throwing away their fruits and vegetables when they are no longer rewarded to eat them.

Without a focus on social infrastructure, better practices simply fade away. Like dozens of people I interviewed, Adelaide, a community food activist living in a lower-income neighborhood in Detroit, expressed grave concern over the "narrowness by which we think about solutions." She highlighted the importance of social infrastructure: "What good is making healthier options more available—or, in the other direction, food taxes or food bans—if people don't know what to do with those foods the powers-that-be deem nutritious, or more sustainable, or more just? It sits on their kitchen counter, or fridge, and never gets eaten— that's what. If you want to create change, you've got to get them to *want* change, and that starts with giving people the tools to experiment with food differently."

What all this points to is the need for a paradigm shift away from narrow medical, educational, and economic models of intervention to broader approaches. After all, we are talking about food here; what aspect of our lives does it not touch? Fortunately, we do not have to look far for inspiration, as there are already communities where this way of thinking is not new but routine.

In 1973, for example, the Community Reinforcement Approach (CRA) was created to rehabilitate alcoholics. Rather than treating the affliction as a personal weakness, solved through prayer, punishment, or reward (which sounds a lot like how we still "treat" unhealthy eating), the CRA refocused attention on an individual's community. The approach recognizes the power of making a sober environment more rewarding than one dominated by alcohol.[12] No longer exclusively a tool for treating substance abuse, community-based frameworks such as Whole School, Whole Community, Whole Child are being developed to address problems involving food.[13] The specifics of these programs are less important than what they have in common: the realization that changing behaviors requires changing communities.

Take the issue of obesity. This phenomenon is especially subject to narrowly conceived models of intervention, whether medical (e.g., gastric bypass), educational (e.g., telling subjects to eat less), or economic (e.g., taxing "bad" foods and subsidizing "good" ones so subjects will eat "better"). As a counterweight, a new field has emerged: civic dietetics. As explained by Mandy, a self-described civic dietician from Denver, Colorado, the field is based on "the recognition that public health, environmental sustainability, agricultural practices, community health, individual well-being, animal welfare, and food justice are all interdependent. Healthy people start with healthy communities." She continued, "Recognizing this admittedly makes our jobs more complicated. Now, we're not just concerned with bodies in a narrow clinical sense—if they're getting enough fiber or vitamin D—but with the broader systems those bodies inhabit. But that's how you get the outcomes you want, which are healthier, happier people. It might be a lot of work, but it's worth it, because the approach works."

Mandy proceeded to map out this approach, drawing from her own experiences. "Communities are built environments that shape what's possible and probable." She began to rearrange her desktop. Pointing to the final product, she continued: "This architecture doesn't dictate, but it does shape and influence how we think and what we do. Where supermarkets are located"—pointing to a stapler on her left—"or farmers' markets or open space for gardens"—now pointing to a notepad on her right side. "All of this shapes consumption patterns, diets." Pointing to two pencils in front of her: "Or, if you want to talk about this architecture in the context of physical activity, where are the parks or bike trails? If the built environment makes physical activity hard to do, people are less likely to do it."

But it's not just the physical environment we ought to pay attention to. This "architecture" includes the less tangible, but equally real, social infrastructure discussed earlier. Mandy explained: "Let's say you want to get healthier food into schools. You've got to engage a lot of levers to do that. One that gets overlooked requires a renegotiation within schools, among administrators and those on school boards especially, of how they think about what's a 'good value'"—she raises her fingers to make air quotes. "To do that you have to lean on social relationships, get those people talking with concerned parents and other stakeholders. It takes a bit of work, but I've been involved in a number of cases where we've gotten those decision makers to really move the needle when it comes to thinking about 'value'"—those fingers again—"from being about cost-minimization to being about healthy food and healthy students."

When people start working together, they are also more likely to overcome barriers that might have seemed insurmountable to individuals. You'll read more about this in the next chapter, where we look at ways to escape the trap set by economies of scale—a.k.a. get big or get out! The point I want to make here is that a community's value cannot be reduced to its financial assets. Instead, its value, what makes it a *desirable* place to live, is an amalgamation of assets: social, cultural, political, built, natural, economic, human, etc. Contrary to what you're taught in Econ 101, market value (e.g., an acre of land for X amount of dollars) is not the only way to measure assets or to accumulate them. Here, then, is a route that avoids conventional pathways, whereby capital and credit are privileged.

Food hubs can take many forms. Generally speaking, they follow the principle of scaling *out* versus scaling up, allowing numerous smaller-scale producers to come together and coordinate their activities. Typically, this begins with the construction of a physical hub, where produce from various farms is brought in and checked for quality, labeled, and kept in cold storage before being distributed to buyers—often schools, college dining halls, senior centers, hospitals, restaurants, and caterers. But in regions with clear growing seasons, an investment to build such a hub can be risky, as that space inevitably sits idle for months, depending on winter's length. Some places, then, are looking at their community's *existing assets* to see what can be bundled, thus avoiding the costly expense of building a specialized hub that lies unused for months on end.

One example can be found in Denver, Colorado. There, farmers, community-development practitioners, and food activists have reached out to downtown businesses and arranged to use their front-entry lobby space as a "hub." Hubs are created from existing community assets, principally social networks and built capital—no nails or hammers required. The strategy not only helps area growers by reducing their cost of entry into the market, which is significant as many smaller-scale farmers are credit- and cash-strapped, but it also gives the employees of these businesses ready access to locally produced food. As for the businesses sharing their lobby space, they too look to benefit. In the words of a manager who okayed this arrangement: "This is a low-cost way to improve employee morale, and it might even make them healthier, too, which benefits us on multiple levels."

CHAPTER 8

Getting Big versus Getting Together

"The little guys have their purpose," Jérémie told me. "But still, the reality is you gotta pay to play. There are efficiencies; if you want to feed the world, there are efficiencies that can only be had with scaling up, with capital investment."

Jérémie works for France's ministry of agriculture, agrifood, and forestry. Our paths crossed in Rome as we were both attending a workshop, hosted by the Food and Agriculture Organization of the United Nations, about global food security. Jérémie works closely with organizations throughout France, trying to implement what he calls "sustainability transitions" among, again in his own words, "mainstream market actors"—large-scale producers, processers, and grocers. His comment came from a conversation we had about the rationale for privileging conventional market actors. His position was that Big Food *has* to exist. "The problems," in his words, "demand solutions that are equally scalable, that are amendable to scaling up with capital investment."

As we reimagine future foodscapes, we need to also re-imagine our economic assumptions. Alas, it is hard to be truly revolutionary if we insist on holding on to the very conventions that got us into the mess we are in. This chapter challenges assumptions about scalability, a.k.a. economies of scale, as understood through the practices of investment and acquisition. Fortunately, this tale speaks more to people's lack of imagination than anything else. Large versus small. Local versus global. Haven't we more options than this? Yes!

The implicit value of scalability, as typically conceived, has been a fixture of economic thought for generations. "Get big or get out!" is a familiar mantra in conventional agricultural circles, dating back to the infamous Earl Butz, secretary of agriculture under Presidents Richard Nixon and Gerald Ford, who made it a constant refrain during his time in office. The times they are a-changing. We now have a viable alternative, thanks to social media, mobile platforms, and the internet—the sharing economy. This chapter describes examples of people choosing to get together rather than get bigger, and it examines the effects of these communities on foodscapes.

"The argument for scalability"—of getting bigger—"is that it reduces costs for the consumer. Firms get big, they say, for consumers; to give them the cheapest product possible." This was Maxine, a UK-based farmer who participates in FarmDrop—a web-based platform designed to provide an alternative distribution model to the conventional market. "What companies are really after," she added, "is market power to extract concessions from those beneath them, from those they buy from. It's all about profitability. Their arguments about efficiency are a ruse. If they were serious about maximizing efficiencies, they'd let themselves go out of business and we'd organize markets differently."

What Maxine is talking about, in economic-speak, is monopsony. Buyer power. Market concentration—getting bigger usually leads to reduced competition as others are forced out of the market—reduces the number of purchasers (meat-packing plants, grain processors, etc.) to the point that sellers (ranchers, farmers, etc.) have few options other than accept the price dictated by the buyer. Want to know why farmers receive pennies on the dollar for the food bought in supermarkets? (Depending on whose calculations you believe, and the commodity in question, conventional producers get between five and forty cents for every dollar spent on food.) It is because they have no choice but to accept such a pittance.

The perishable nature of what they produce leaves farmers in an especially precarious position. This is particularly true for meat and dairy producers. Those raising livestock rely on selling their animals the moment they reach optimum weight. Feeding animals beyond that point is a waste of feed, space (that poop has to go somewhere), and resources. In the case of hogs, a timely sale is essential to clear room for the next litter. For dairy producers, the bulk tank must be emptied daily, sometimes several times a day. All of these realities make it difficult for producers to hold out for a better price; unlike when you post furniture for sale on Craigslist, food values can drop appreciably from one day to the next. To make matters worse, livestock producers face constraints that generally limit them to nearby markets, so seeking out competitive bids from faraway buyers is unrealistic. Shipping live animals long distances can be prohibitively expensive. It also increases animal mortality rates and carcass shrinkage: more reasons distant markets are a bad bet for most livestock producers, not to mention the animals themselves.

Another important component of the power imbalance is the rise of contract farming. In livestock production, where contracts are most widely used, the contractors—processing firms—own the animals. The farmers, meanwhile, are responsible for building and managing the facilities, usually to the contractors' specifications. In turn, the farmers receive all inputs from the buyers—feed, veterinary services, and transportation when it is time for the animals to be slaughtered. This might sound like an equitable relationship, until you factor in for those aforementioned market asymmetries.

While processors have their pick of producers, farmers rarely have more than one or two buyers from whom to obtain a contract. Producers lack leverage in negotiating these contracts because they lack exit power—the power to walk away from the negotiating table, knowing others are out there to purchase their product. Contracts—all contracts, I might add—benefit parties with leverage, which in contract agriculture are not the farmers. Chicken producers, for example, can invest as much as $1,000,000 in facilities that have a twenty- to thirty-year life with no practical alternative use. Once such a facility is built, the producer is under tremendous pressure to obtain and maintain their contract with processors, no matter how unfairly it might be structured.

This brings me back to Maxine's earlier point about how "arguments about efficiency" by Big Food "are a ruse." *Efficiency* in this context simply means greater profits for industry. To rephrase General Motors' famous slogan, what's good for big business may *not* be good for everyone else. These efficiencies are certainly not good for most farmers. If they were, do you think we would have lost two-thirds of them in the United States over the last century? (The number of American farms dropped from more than 6 million in 1935 to roughly 2 million in 2012.) Average US farm incomes have steadily been on the decline for generations—dropping 36 percent in 2015 alone.[1] What about the bottom line of communities—*all* the assets mentioned in the previous chapter? As farms, people, and profits disappear from the countryside, poverty and social isolation take their place. And the planet? It is popular to talk about the "Three P's" of sustainability—People, Planet, and Profits: the idea that practices must be socially sustainable, environmentally sustainable, and economically sustainable for them to work in the long term. Big Food's actions certainly fail from an environmental sustainability standpoint—consider monocultures, chickens with over-sized breasts, and beef cows fed a steady diet of therapeutic antibiotics. And yet, the sector is routinely hailed for its "efficiencies."[2]

But the consumers! Let's not forget about them. These cost-squeezing strategies benefit them. You're not against cheap food, are you?

I hear this argument a lot, from proponents of the status quo, especially when they're backed into a corner. But here is the problem with it. Individuals are not just consumers. They are also citizens. Which is to say, they do not just buy stuff, they also have lives outside retail markets, filled with families, loved ones, interests, and passions. They might have a family member who is, or was, a farmer. They undoubtedly live in a community, somewhere, perhaps in a rural community grappling with poverty and community disintegration. They also live on this planet and they probably do not want to see it turn to shit—that's my response to large-scale industrial livestock production. And, like it or not, we're all taxpayers and members of a social contract. Lest we forget, many of these "efficiencies" will eventually have to be cleaned up with taxpayer dollars, from the animal effluent in our waterways to the obesity epidemic that results from industry's unwillingness to pay its laborers a livable wage—obesity rates are positively correlated with poverty.

Community-based food initiatives, until recently, have largely needed eaters who were ready to sacrifice some level of convenience for their values. This is not to dismiss the hard work by activists up until this point. Any revolution begins with people working together, sacrificing time and energy for a cause they believe in. But eventually, unless we want to base our future foodscapes on notions of sacrifice, we are going to need to make it convenient for people to participate in these more civic-minded foodscapes. The good news is that we do not have to look far for examples of people creating "markets" that look nothing like those dominated by Big Food, and without all those aforementioned costs either.

FarmDrop, mentioned earlier, is a London-based startup founded by former Morgan Stanley stockbroker Ben Pugh in 2012. Pugh's mission has been to restructure the food supply chain by removing the intermediaries that currently separate consumers and producers, thus giving farmers a fairer financial deal without hitting consumers' pocketbooks. It seems to be working. Producers receive an average of 70 percent of the sales revenue through FarmDrop (even higher for commodities like milk: 80 percent), while eaters get access to food that is priced competitively with what they would find at their grocery store. Factor in the free home delivery (on orders of more than £25) and the fact that you are receiving vegetables that have been picked and breads that have been baked the same day as they are delivered, and the price-competitiveness is undeniable.

According to the company, the average distance between the customer and the producer of the food sold through this arrangement is thirty miles. As of late 2015, roughly seventy producers supply goods to FarmDrop, which uses electric vans within three zones across London to make deliveries. The company also aims for transparency. Its website lists where each of its products comes from, along with extensive biographies of all affiliated producers, from farmers to bakers, pasta makers, and fisher-persons.

"The goal of alternative distribution models like The Food Assembly, FarmDrop, and the Open Food Network is about increasing transparency, giving people the tools to know where their food comes from while creating new distribution channels—so new, in fact, that they bypass conventional supply chains entirely," said Jen, a small-scale farmer and baker with ties to the Open Food Network Australia—another internet-based platform, in some respects like FarmDrop, to connect producers and consumers. "It's important to realize just how revolutionary these new platforms have the potential of being," she added. "The argument that you need to get bigger is an outmoded one. Getting bigger means creating market distortions"—remember what I said earlier about monopsony. "It's about putting the little guys out of business, failing to realize that those small businesses help create vibrant communities and neighborhoods, and help households stay afloat financially. Why bother getting big? Getting together is far more optimal for everyone involved."

Even among these alternative platforms there are degrees of alternative-ness, if you will forgive the clunky terminology. Jen mentioned the Open Food Network in the same breath as FarmDrop. On the surface, these tools look remarkably similar. Both are web-based platforms designed to cut out intermediaries and reduce the distance, social and spatial, between eaters and producers. You have to know what you are looking for in order the spot the differences between them: subtle disparities that could easily be overlooked, but which have the potential to produce quite different outcomes.

Founded by Serenity Hill and Kirsten Larsen out of Melbourne, Australia, the Open Food Network is built on free and open-source software. FarmDrop, conversely, is a proprietary platform developed with the help of crowdfunding as well as a number of significant individual investments. FarmDrop is therefore not cutting out the middleman entirely, but standing in for traditional intermediaries. Its frequently advertised revenue split is 80/10/10: 80 percent to those who raise and make the food; 10 percent to "keepers"—namely, those who manage the online platform and encourage membership; and 10 percent to Farm-Drop. Some of that 20 percent not going to producers ends up in the pockets of investors, though I was not able to find out precisely how much. FarmDrop is also a standardized alternative, which is to say that its look, its functionality, and the platform and code it is built on are fixed, which is a common feature of any proprietary technology—think Microsoft Office.

The Open Food Network, by contrast, and to quote Jen, "grows by sharing ideas, creating a space for all stakeholders, and redesigning code according to whatever comes out of those deliberative processes. It's about the creation of community-based ventures, for communities and according to their needs and resources." Because the Open Food Network is based on open-source code, it is decidedly not standardized, which underscores Jen's point about how the platform allows communities to "redesign" it "for communities and according to their needs and resources." Thus, unlike FarmDrop, which is a private proprietary company controlled by its founders, Open Source Network is *freeing*.

Talking to growers, I was also unable come up with a clear revenue breakdown like FarmDrop's advertised 80/10/10 split. "That's not dictated by the platform," Jen told me when I asked her about this. "That's left up to each community to decide. This isn't a for-profit venture, so it's not like the original code developers are looking to get their cut." This brings me to the issue of farmer autonomy. FarmDrop is undeniably equitable, in the sense that it funnels far more of every dollar spent on food back to producers than conventional supply chains do. Yet we cannot ignore that farmers remain beholden to key market actors in this arrangement, namely, FarmDrop itself. FarmDrop still dictates prices, whereas in the Open Food Network the question of who sets prices is part of the conversation.

There was also some concern among producers linked to FarmDrop that the aforementioned 80/10/10 split could change. What if its investors eventually decide that returns are insufficient? FarmDrop holds sufficient leverage to demand a larger cut of revenue. As long as producers are promised a larger share than what is offered through conventional supply chains, they will have to accept whatever FarmDrop tells them is fair. I am not saying this will happen. The people I talked to who were associated with this platform seemed genuine in their concerns about returning as large a share as possible back to producers. My point is simply that the platform itself does not really *empower* producers—enriching and empowering are not necessarily the same things. As one grower quipped, "Fortunately, they"— FarmDrop—"are proving to be far kinder and gentler than actors in conventional markets. But that could change."

I met Markus while participating in a workshop sponsored by the US Federal Reserve Bank of St. Louis. Markus is a community development specialist with a keen interest in phenomena that fall under the umbrella of collaborative consumption, also known as the sharing economy. It is an interest that has taken him around the United States, meeting entrepreneurs who want to, in his words, "apply principles of the sharing economy to food systems." My travels have also introduced me to a number of people reimagining foodscapes through this lens, where sharing, collaboration, and getting together substitute for buying, consumer sovereignty, and getting bigger. So we spent a good bit of our conversation comparing notes: what we've seen, and where; what worked and what didn't; who benefited and who didn't. "Collaborative consumption has totally disrupted business as usual," Markus remarked, reflecting on what he has seen while crisscrossing the country. "Under the old model, it is all about buying, building, and bullying. No longer. Now we're talking about access and resources, as opposed to just resources."

Aristotle is said to have written that "on the whole, you find wealth much more in use than in ownership."[3] Echoing this sentiment, Kevin Kelly, founder of the influential magazine *Wired,* has argued that "access is better than ownership."[4] We have become so wrapped up in ownership—buy, Buy, BUY!—that we have forgotten why we want to own things in the first place: for access and use.

When given the opportunity to lecture on collaborative consumption, I always survey audiences about the things they own but rarely use. Recently I had almost every audience member, in a group of more than 200, raise a hand when asked who owns a power drill. "Okay, now keep your hand up if you've used that drill in the last six months," I then instructed. Only twenty-one hands remained up. The rest, more than 100 drills, were sitting idle in various closets, basements, or garages. That's a tremendous amount of idle hole-making capacity; lest we forget, we don't own drills for their own sake but for *access* to what drills can do.

Enough about drills and holes. Back to food.

A pilot project in Colorado is in the works to connect aspirational food entrepreneurs—cooks, chefs, and bakers, principally—with idle kitchen space with the help of a web-based platform. Like other peer-to-peer (P2P) networks, such as FarmDrop and the Open Food Network, this platform aims to grow regional food-system capacity by building on existing idle and thus underutilized resources—remember the conversation at the end of the last chapter about sharing community assets. Under the old model, which, according to Markus, promotes "buying, building, and bullying," upstart food entrepreneurs require significant amounts of capital and credit if they ever hope to access conventional distribution channels. This creates insurmountable barriers to entry, save for those with ready access to considerable financial resources. In other words, the current model of entrepreneurialism, where economic capital and credit are privileged, and all those other community assets are ignored, encourages more of the same.

Historically, the transaction costs of making these connections, between those wanting access and those in possession of idle assets, were too great. Thanks to the internet, smartphones, and global-positioning-satellite (GPS) technology, those with idle kitchen space—or drills, cars, bedrooms, etc.—and those wanting to use such resources can now be connected with just a few taps on one's iPhone.

"This is about making better use of a community's assets. Not just certain assets, *all* of them," said Lana, a rural development specialist with the USDA. "Communities are rich in assets," she added, "but we tend to privilege economic ones because we haven't been good at bringing those other types together. That's beginning to change."

In the case of the web-based platform that connects aspiring chefs and cooks with idle kitchen space, as with most P2P models, we see the substitution of social capital (social networks) and built capital (idle kitchen space, the internet, etc.) for financial capital (money to build new kitchen space).[5] In other words, and for those who recoil at policy-wonk-speak, we are seeing in alternative foodscapes a reevaluation of all community-based assets. This perspective is an antidote to the idea that only money can solve a community's ills, food-based or otherwise, and such new thinking is encouraging if indeed it is true that, as noted in the prior chapter, money primes people to act selfishly and to look inward. The cook who needs commercial kitchen space to live out a dream—let's say, to use an actual example, scaling up production of Grandma's jam recipe—can now find it, for a reasonable price. (And we're talking about access to serious commercial equipment in some cases, such as what's available at schools and community centers.) This model makes it easier for "the little guys" to enter conventional markets or, better yet, alternative markets, such as those made possible through P2P platforms like FarmDrop and the Open Food Network.

I met Bernie through a mutual acquaintance. "You've got to get in contact with this guy," my friend kept telling me. "He belongs to this community, Farm Hack. He'll have to tell you about it." Farm Hack? Yep, I thought to myself, I need to talk to this guy.

As described on the group's website, "[We are] a worldwide community of farmers that build and modify our own tools. We share our hacks online and at meet-ups because we become better farmers when we work together."[6] As Bernie told me shortly after I met him, "We used to be able to fix damn near anything with spit and sweat, a couple bungee cords, and bailing wire." We met in his machine shed. To the untrained eye it might have looked like a place where old equipment went to die, a glorified indoor junkyard. But I knew better. Growing up in rural Iowa teaches you a couple things, one being the ability to spot classic farm equipment and parts—I spied, for example, a dusty but complete 1945 John Deere Model D tractor hiding behind a pile of logs. He continued, "Not anymore. Now, when my combine or tractor breaks down—*mine*, mind you, I own it—but when it breaks down I not only can't fix it, I'm not even legally *allowed* to, even if I could, which I can't."

By design, there is a lot of dependence under the dominant model. Recall the comment about how the current paradigm encourages "buying, building, and bullying"—bullying, a blunter way of saying dependency. I have already mentioned the example of contract farming and market asymmetries that make farmers subservient to buyers—monopsony. Bernie was describing another form of dependency, namely, farmer reliance on dealers' and manufacturers' technicians. The (US) Digital Millennium Copyright Act, passed in 1998 to prevent digital piracy, declares it a breach of copyright to break a technological protection—to break into, in other words, a tractor's engine control unit (tECU)—essentially the brains of any "smart" piece of farming equipment. That is what Bernie meant when he said he is not "even legally allowed to fix" his equipment.

There is a distinct sense of unease in the Farm Hack community about losing practical knowledge and becoming ever more dependent.[7] Farmers take great pride in being a DIY (Do It Yourself) group. Bernie stands visibly taller when he speaks of fixing "damn near anything with spit and sweat, a couple bungee cords, and bailing wire." That is becoming increasingly difficult, in part because it is increasingly becoming illegal to do so. As farmers lose that hard-won DIY knowledge, they also lose a large measure of control, not to mention sense of self.

This is where Farm Hack comes into the picture. Started in 2010, Farm Hack seeks to "set farmers free," in the words of Wally, another Farm Hack member. "We encourage farmers to purchase analog"—in other words, non-computerized—"farming implements that they can actually fix without having a master's degree in computer science and a password that only John Deere knows." Wally went on to tell me about the Slow Tools Project, like the solar-powered "horse tractor" for regions of the world dependent on draft animals, and the sensor system designed with open-source code for recording the temperature and moisture of active compost. "Farming is in my blood," he added. "That way of life is being taken away from me by corporations who are more interested in profiting off of me than anything. First they made us farm out of cans"—a reference to farmers' dependence on agro-industrial inputs. "Now we're literally someone who just pushes buttons, and we can't even fix the buttons when they've broke. I feel like I'm in a straight-jacket. Farm Hack sets farmers free."

To quote Kevin, speaking about the Farm Hack community: "We're a living repository of knowledge. If we don't manage anything other than to help future farmers remember how to fix equipment, we've done our jobs, because they're starting to forget." Chapter 1 discussed the phenomenon of collective forgetting, describing how conventional foodscapes induce a type of shared amnesia about food, on both the production and consumption ends. Farm Hack is determined to help its community remember.

Meanwhile, there is also the issue of practical knowledge *missed* under current arrangements. We have to be careful not to romanticize farmers as only understanding and being capable of understanding analog technologies. The yeomen farmers of yesteryear are just that, a nostalgic image with very little resemblance to the growers and ranchers I know. Some of those I interviewed acknowledged the value of circulating *digital* information among networks as another way of reducing farmer dependency on firms and "approved" service providers.

Barb, for example, has extensive computer experience. She is also a farmer, in addition to being, in her words, "loosely affiliated with Farm Hack but fully behind the spirit of what it stands for." She has created agriculture-based open-source code, such as crop-planning software that allows users to develop planting schedules, estimate yields, and calculate seed and fertilizer needs. Her interest in "smart" agriculture technology, however, does not stop there: "The DIY, open-source, and small-scale poly-crop movements are coming together to develop their own version of 'precision agriculture,' like FarmBot"—an invention that was a finalist for the prestigious Hackaday Prize in 2015. (FarmBot looks like a 3D printer hovering above soil, but instead of constructing something made of plastic it uses its injectors to expel seeds, water, and fertilizer.) She went on to explain how "smart technology doesn't have to be alienating" and added that "too often those of us critical of Big Ag are painted as being anti-technology—crazy back-to-the-landers. We shouldn't be afraid of technology. It doesn't have to be alienating if we develop it together."

It doesn't have to be alienating if we develop it together: in other words, the specific technology we use is not as important as how that technology connects us. Later in the interview, Barb explained how she "enjoys getting together with other farmers and teaching them about software, and when they're really eager we talk about things like programming language"—an example of doing code together. "And it's incredibly rewarding for me—helping them find ways to become part of this broader community while simultaneously freeing them from the grips of companies like John Deere."

CHAPTER 9
Becoming Citizens

It's easy to suggest solutions when you don't know too much about the problem. That's particularly true of food, which involves problems that can be maddeningly complex. Complex, however, does not mean impossible. No panaceas, of course. Education; external incentives; food bans; Green Revolutions: one-size-fits-all approaches ignore the truth that the only worthwhile solutions are those that people find themselves. This leads me to offer this one observation, the closest I'll come to a magic bullet, which unites the wide array of alternative-foodscape inhabitants quoted throughout this book. They all express a desire to create citizens rather than just consumers.

"We just can't rely upon the same strategies as in other industries to increase purchase frequency. While people can buy bigger houses or rent garage space for more stuff, their stomachs are only so big." I was interviewing Sam, who at one time oversaw the North American marketing for a division of a major food company. We were talking about consumer choice: what it means, how it is constructed, and how firms use it to their advantage. Sam continued: "We talk about how choice is good for consumers. In truth, manufactures are the ones benefiting most from it." Hanging on the wall to Sam's right was a collage (a gift from his daughter, I later learned) displaying dozens of different products whose "lives" he helped oversee during his tenure as senior executive. Sam pointed to it more than once during our conversation, as when the subject turned to how industry uses choice to drive overconsumption: "If you give people enough choices they'll actually buy more than they need. Why? Because too much choice leads to regret, regret of what wasn't bought. So they'll end up buying more."

That's right, forget the myth that consumer choice improves our lives. We have been misled. Consumer choice: a source of remorse over what was not bought. Sam's remarks square with the consumer psychological literature.[1] Want people to overconsume? Give them many choices, or at least the illusion of plenty. Chances are good they will end up buying more than they need to avoid those pangs of regret. And even then, misery still—depression, perhaps obesity. Let's not forget, we are talking about the overconsumption of food.

I wanted to hear more about Sam's take on choice, and he obliged.

"I think for us, for those of us in industry, it is what you would expect: option maximization. And fortunately for us, having all these options work in our favor, at least when it comes to getting consumers to *over*consume." Then it appeared, a crack in the façade of choice, when he allowed himself to question the position that consumers generate meaningful social change through shopping, by "voting" with their dollars. Remember, they may be voting, but, as with American electoral politics at the national level, what are you really voting for when your choices are Coke or Pepsi—no offense intended to either brand in equating them with the two major US political parties. Sam

conceded, "But I'll admit that it's debatable if having twenty different potato chips to choose from is really choice, especially when those
twenty flavors come from one or two companies. But that's where we
come in"—*we* being those in the advertising biz—"to make it look like
the choices are real."

"What are you telling me, that those choices are not real? That they're
a mirage?" I asked.

"It's not that choice is a mirage," Sam answered. Pausing long to produce a cocksure grin, he added, "It's just what we make it to be."

Choice: *It's just what we make it to be.* This might sound like some
nonsensical postmodern quip, as in "Your choice is what I say it is."
My point is that the concept does not exist in isolation. That was Sam's
point, too: our grasp of "choice" is based on a broader social environment that gives the concept a particular feel, and that feel can vary
across foodscapes.

Sam was not the only one who expressed such attitudes. Take those
articulated by Jeff, who at the time was employed by a New York–based
advertising agency. In recent years, Jeff oversaw a number of projects
requiring his team to increase the "purchasing frequency"—his words—
of certain snack items. "I'm sometimes worried," he admitted, "at how
successful we've been. People can be plopped in the middle of a food
desert, nothing but 7-Eleven, McDonald's, White Castle, and Church's
Chicken as far as the eye can see, and they think they're surrounded by
some grand panoply of choice." And why do we equate choice with a
bunch of products nearly identical in their tastes, supply chains, and
corporate structures? (I recently walked into a 7-Eleven to see how
many of their packaged snacks—chips and crackers, that sort of stuff—
are owned by PepsiCo: *70 percent.*) Jeff's response: "A lot of time and
resources are being spent holding that image of 'choice' together."

Actually, there is more than time and money holding that image
together. There is also history.

There are global consequences to current taste preferences—diets based on roughly ten plants, certain animal parts, and fruits and vegetables with picture perfect looks. I am often asked if we can feed the world sustainably. That depends, I always respond, on what we mean by *feed*. Do we mean feeding the world with only perfectly straight carrots, unblemished monochromatic tomatoes and apples, borer-free sweet corn, and with bananas that conform to our aesthetic ideal? Do we think stomachs ought to be oblivious to seasons and regions, like those stomachs in high-income countries where they can be filled with "fresh" fruits and vegetables year-round from six of the world's seven continents? Are we content with future generations living primarily off processed foods, recognizing that, thanks to the Green Revolution, most of these "foods" are better described as agro-industrial inputs—corn, soybeans, wheat, and rice. There is not a lot you can do with many of these cereal grains and legumes, particularly the handful of varieties grown ubiquitously today, other than process them. And meat: when we talk about future food "needs," just how much do we have in mind? What about particular cuts of animal flesh? Our exclusive tastes are distorting, as I have already detailed—remember the repeated references to chickens with giant breasts in the chapter 6. Among countries, the king of carnivores is Luxembourg, consuming roughly 136 kilograms (300 pounds) of meat per person per year, which breaks down pretty evenly between cow, pig, and chicken, with a little left over for sheep and "other." If everyone in the world consumed meat at that level, there would only be enough grain remaining to support a global population of about 2.6 billion people.[2] Are all countries hoping to mimic the Luxembourg diet? I sure hope not.

So yes, we can feed the world sustainably, but getting there is going to require some work. Changing practices is never easy. And consumers can't do it alone. They can choose, for example, the GMO-free Santitas Tortilla Chips over MSG-free Doritos Tortilla Chips, but they are still buying a PepsiCo product. How's that "change"? Eaters' real power lies in their role as citizens, working together. That is the only way we can counter the weight of history—with a weight of our own, a collective mass.

History? Weight? I am going somewhere with these terms. The concept I have in mind comes from institutional economics; yes, even some branches of economics understand that the ghost of consumer sovereignty is just that, an aberration. I am thinking about what is known as path dependency,[3] the idea that we get "locked in" to particular ways of doing things and thus get "locked out" of alternatives.

The classic example is the "QWERTY" keyboard arrangement—we're straying from food for a moment, but your patience will be rewarded. This arrangement, found on keyboards throughout the world, is not the most efficient. Far from it: even though most typists are right-handed, the QWERTYUIOP arrangement makes one's left hand perform 56 percent of the work; 48 percent of the time just one hand is used, as in the word *addressed*; and finger dexterity is not linked to letter frequency. This was a virtue decades ago, when typewriters were still of the "clickety-clack . . . ding" variety with their ink ribbons and mechanical arms. Those arms jam if you type fast enough. Early mechanical typewriters were intentionally designed to slow the most efficient typists down just enough to avoid these mishaps. You might think that we would have adopted a more efficient configuration over the years, especially once mechanical typewriters gave way first to electric typewriters and then to word processors and then to personal computers, tablets, and smartphones. But we have not. Think about the initial costs of such a switch. Proficient typists would cease to be so proficient, at least until they mastered the new configuration. And computer companies—where is their incentive to switch? They could offer consumers an alternative configuration, but who would buy it? No one, not until we have changed the ingrained habits that reproduce how we type. (Curiously, new mobile platforms, with their different key configuration, might be doing just that—proof that locks can be picked!) So if it takes work to get unstuck from our "need" for the QWERTY, just think of the collective effort required to get unstuck from the dominant foodscape. Software to "remap" keyboards is widely available, after all, while acquiring alternative foodscapes takes a heck of a lot more than a Google search. Today's eaters are effectively locked into particular choices, even though better alternatives exist.

Just remember, though—all locks can be picked. Or kicked in.

Stephanie is a food scientist who has spent most of her twenty-year career working for various cereal divisions of international food companies. During one point in our conversation, the topic of consumer choice came up. "We make batches that make tens, even hundreds, or thousands of servings. We also have to make sure that what we're making is sufficiently stable so it will withstand the wild temperature changes of transportation, especially from the store to the consumer's house—in the summer it could be sitting in a 120-degree [Fahrenheit] car. To meet the needs of the industrialization process and long-distance commodity chains mean we're"—she's referring to food scientists here—"working within shared parameters."

I have heard points like this repeatedly from industry insiders, about how, to quote another respondent, "the industrial process precludes a number of foods, which means it also precludes certain tastes, sensations, and textures." Later this food scientist, Steve, added, "Just look at what apples or tomatoes are available at your local grocery store. The ones you see are the ones that can handle the industrialization process. But that's just a fraction of what's actually out there. That's what I mean when I say the industrialization process flattens out the tastes and experiences available to consumers."

Far-reaching claims: "the industrialization process *flattens out the tastes and experiences* available to consumers" (Steve) and "to meet the needs of the industrialization process and long-distance commodity chains means we're all sort of *working within shared parameters*" (Stephanie). What, then, becomes of those foods, and the foodscapes whence they came, that fall outside those parameters? They are forgotten—that collective amnesia discussed in prior chapters.

The good news is that we are remembering. The alternative foodscapes popping up around the world are powerful, and hopeful, because the change they seek is not superficial, not like changing from one PepsiCo chip to another. Instead, they allow us to reimagine our core beliefs about food, like how we understand "choice." Take the following quote from Tara, an eater in Italy who is part of a Solidarity Purchasing Group (*Gruppi di Acquisto Solidale* in Italian). (When a food purchasing group puts people and environment before profit it becomes a *solidarity* purchasing group. Groups are typically composed of friends and neighbors who pool their buying power and purchase collectively from ethically responsible local, organic, small-scale producers.) "The more you become involved in these alternative food networks, the more you begin to rethink really fundamental stuff. When I think about choice, now, after being active in these networks for years, I can't image how I ever thought the conventional system provided me with any."

Or take this comment, from a grower living outside of London who supplies vegetables and fruits for London-area restaurants: "This is all about choice, everyone doing their part to create a different system—farmers, field hands, restaurant owners, servers, wait staff, consumers. We all have to choose change and believe in a different way of feeding society."

Or this one, from an Austrian farmer who is active in the international movement *La Vía Campesina*: "We're interested in giving people an alternative to the Green Revolution and industrial agriculture. It's really about expanding the choices out there for farmers and peasants—for everyone really, because everyone eats."

For Big Food, an aisle of potato chips is the definition of choice, even though every bag came from a handful of firms with essentially identical supply chains that all reach back to the same two or three Goliath-size potato growers. Yet choice, as the comments above make clear, does not have to look that way. What if we had far fewer potato chip options, but each variety supported different farmers, laborers, and communities? Many challenging the food status quo are open to reducing our choices as consumers in order to increase our choices as citizens. Citizens, of course, have many more obligations than just making sure they get the best deal. We are talking here about prioritizing citizenship over consumption.

Is this a crazy notion? No crazier than surrendering to what economist Alfred Kahn has aptly called the "tyranny of small decisions"—Coke or Pepsi?—when we could be using that time to build strong, vibrant, and just communities and households. Lisa perhaps put it best, this distinction between consumer and citizen choice, when she said, "I get irked when people claim we're against consumer choice. That's not true at all. We are against the *illusion* of choice you get in a supermarket. We want more choice. But a choice that brings people and communities together and that helps sustain the environment; not a choice that locks us into practices that collectively makes us less well off."

Nancy, an artisanal cheese maker located on New Zealand's South Island, made almost identical remarks when telling me how she's "tired of hearing that people looking to make a change to our food system are limiting options; that we're about telling people what they can't do; that we're asking consumers to somehow sacrifice." Then, looking at me with a mixture of sadness and exasperation, she added, "That's shit. I've seen it a hundred times if I've seen it once. Once people learn how to select fresh foods and prepare them, once they have a taste for them, once they've formed social ties with other eaters and producers, and as long as the foods are affordable and accessible, they'll choose the food system I'm a part of 99 times out of 100."

Well said, Nancy—profanities and all. The truly revolutionary food-scapes are not interested in dictating what we can and cannot have, even though they are often accused of it. Rather, they are working to open up our worlds by offering us the tools, knowledge, skills, and feelings to want—to *choose*—a different tomorrow. The specifics of that future are not predetermined, other than that they allow us to be citizens first.

"Picture a pasture open to all."[4] So begins a tale—a fairytale, it turns out—told to scare us into believing there really is a bogeyman: selfish little old us. I am talking about Garrett Hardin's classic essay, "The Tragedy of the Commons." The story continues:

> It is to be expected that each herdsman will try to keep as many cattle as possible on the commons. Such an arrangement may work reasonably satisfactorily for centuries because tribal wars, poaching, and disease keep the numbers of both man and beast well below the carrying capacity of the land. Finally, however, comes the day of reckoning, that is, the day when the long-desired goal of social stability becomes a reality. At this point, the inherent logic of the commons remorselessly generates tragedy.[5]

Assuming that each herdswoman wishes to maximize her gain, she begins to ponder the consequences of adding one more animal to the herd. She soon realizes that the costs and benefits of such an action are unevenly distributed. The herdsperson receives all the proceeds from the sale of the additional animal, while everyone shares the effects of overgrazing. It is therefore perfectly rational for, and therefore to be expected that, herdspersons in this situation will continually add animals to their herd—*all* herdspersons. Therein lies the tragedy: everyone acting in their own self-interest, when resources are shared and limited, will have catastrophic ends. This led Hardin to conclude, famously, and bleakly, "Freedom in a commons brings ruin to all."[6]

Hardin's essay, while provocative, makes a fatal omission: namely, that people, especially those in the same community, interact with one another—they talk, love, laugh, trust, and share "more than we can tell" knowledge. This obvious fact—seriously, how do people continue to miss it?—ought to show us all that *homo economicus* (economic human), a purely rational, selfish person who single-mindedly strives to maximize profit, is no more real than a unicorn. Decades of social science research documents how repeated face-to-face interaction can, over time, build social capital, trust, and empathy and rein in the type of egoistic behavior described in Hardin's essay.[7] When individuals are placed in a situation where they cannot communicate with others, they are indeed more likely to act selfishly. The moment they are allowed to communicate, however, they begin to think more about what is best for the collective and less in terms of their individual interests.[8]

Just to be clear, I am not arguing against markets per se. But we need to realize that markets can take different forms. They can exist outside formal distribution channels, as in the case of FarmDrop. They need not be single-mindedly competitive but can instead share resources, as in the case of Farm Hack and the Open Food Network. There is an enormous difference between having market economies and being a market society. The former is rooted in stakeholder involvement, inclusiveness, trust, empathy, and friendship. The latter is premised on dependency and exclusiveness (thanks to market asymmetries as well as ever-widening social distance), social isolation, intrinsic values, and a general selfishness.

A market society also creates barriers to collective action by increasing the transaction costs of getting together. It shapes, for example, whom we interact with and the aims of those interactions. Thanks to social distance, we are not only physically separated from "Others" but cut off from them emotionally, linguistically, and culturally as well, which is why getting such groups together makes people uncomfortable.

Economist Albert Hirschman, in his brilliant treatise *Exit, Voice, and Loyalty*, argues that people generally have two basic choices when they are unhappy.[9] They can either leave the situation or they can protest and give voice to their troubles. In the conventional marketplace—and in a market society—exit becomes the primary, and often the only, available response to displeasure. If you do not like a particular brand of popcorn, you stop buying it. If a brand of socks irritates your skin, you buy from a competitor instead. If an ice cream parlor repeatedly shorts you on scoops, you stop going there. The marketplace makes exit easy, but at the expense of voice. Ever try complaining about a product or service? I have. My experience is probably familiar to anyone with a cell phone. I call the cell company, stay on hold for thirty minutes, never get to express my concerns, and eventually hang up to tend to my crying son in the next room.

In social relationships, exit is the response of last resort—for good reason, as it is a highly ineffective way to communicate displeasure if the aim is to make things better. When someone exits the marketplace, it could be for any number of reasons, such as death, unemployment, or a change in diet. Or, in the case of a friend of mine, divorce: he changed ketchup brands after separating from his partner, as his old brand reminded him of her. Even when exit is the result of genuine displeasure, without voice there is no way to figure out *why* someone left. So much for the idea that conventional markets are some grand arbiter of choice. How can they know what people want if they are *uninterested* in listening and unaware that there are voices they should be listening *to*?

By now this point should be clear and uncontroversial: foodscapes are not just about what we eat. If you think otherwise, your well-intentioned solutions will always come up short. Being a responsible eater is about more than consumption—even conscious consumption. As detailed throughout this book, we cannot expect today's social ills, food-based and otherwise (as everything is connected), to be addressed exclusively through markets, even more just ones. Which is why my call all along has been for us to work together. Social change, *real* social change, can only come through our actions as citizen-eaters, which include but are not limited to buying.

Citizen-eaters? By this, I do not simply mean people with the legal status of citizenship, signifying membership in a state. I mean people who *act* as citizens, whose actions have the potential to make a real difference—it's important to note that undocumented immigrants can be, and in many cases are, citizen-eaters. Before going any further, I need to distinguish between *active* and *activist* citizens.[10] Citizenship likely calls to mind activities such as voting, volunteering, donating money to charities and community organizations, writing letters to the editor, signing petitions, even voting with your pocketbook—acts, I also realize, that are made easier by financial means. Many of these acts support established social practices and conventions. While important from the standpoint of nurturing civic health, active citizenship doesn't tend to stimulate revolution. Activist citizens, by contrast, challenge the status quo, which makes their endeavor political rather than politics as usual.

No One Eats Alone explores spaces that encourage active and especially activist citizens—citizen-eaters. That's what we need, no more, no less: political participation, community action, and a willingness to be uncomfortable, as breaking from a routine is unnerving, especially when getting to know "Others" that populate foodscapes. The choice is ours: more of the same or an alternative, which is less a predetermined endpoint than an invitation to come together in order to create something different.

The seeds of change are all around us. And they're beginning to take root and sprout.

Notes

Introduction

1. The Hartman Group. 2012. "Eating Alone: The Food Marketer's Hidden Opportunity," *Hartbeat News,* October 17, http://www.hartman-group.com/hartbeat/446/eating-alone-the-food-marketer-s-hidden-opportunity.
2. Wollan, Malia. 2016. "Failure to Lunch: The Lamentable Rise of Desktop Dining," *New York Times Magazine,* February 25, http://www.nytimes.com/2016/02/28/magazine/failure-to-lunch.html?_r=0.
3. As some of the topics discussed in this book are sensitive, I promised respondents anonymity in order to encourage forthright conversations, so pseudonyms are used when individuals are quoted.

Chapter 1

1. I have covered the topic of the Green Revolution extensively in previous books. See, for example: Carolan, Michael. 2011. *The Real Cost of Cheap Food.* New York; London: Earthscan/Routledge; Carolan, Michael. 2013. *Reclaiming Food Security.* New York; London: Earthscan/Routledge.
2. Thompson, Carol. 2007. "Africa: Green Revolution or Rainbow Evolution?" *Foreign Policy in Focus* 17, July, www.fpif.org/articles/africa_green_revolution_or_rainbow_evolution, accessed August 11, 2016.
3. "George," personal interview, January 21, 2014.
4. Orwell, George. 1992 (1949). *1984.* New York: Random House, 260.
5. Connerton, Paul. 1989. *How Societies Remember.* Cambridge, UK: Cambridge University Press, 13–14.

6. Kilman, Scott, and Roger Thurow. 2009. "Father of the Green Revolution Dies," *Wall Street Journal,* September 13, http://online.wsj.com/news/articles/SB125281643150406425?mg=reno64-wsj&url=http%3A%2F%2Fonline.wsj.com%2Farticle%2FSB125281643150406425.html, accessed August 11, 2016.

7. Polanyi, Michael. 1966. *The Tacit Dimension.* New York: Doubleday, Garden City, NY, 4.

8. Gorenfloa, L., S. Romaineb, R. Mittermeierc, and K. Walker-Painemilla. 2012. "Co-occurrence of Linguistic and Biological Diversity in Biodiversity Hotspots and High Biodiversity Wilderness Areas," *PNAS* 109 (21): 8032–37.

9. Nazarea, Virginia. 2005. *Heirloom Seeds and Their Keepers: Marginality and Memory in the Conservation of Biological Diversity.* Tucson, AZ: University of Arizona Press.

10. Ibid., 62.

11. Ibid.

12. Smale, Melinda, Mauricio Bellon, and Jose Gomez. 2001. "Maize Diversity, Variety Attributes, and Farmers' Choices in Southeastern Guanajuato, Mexico," *Economic Development and Cultural Change* 50: 201–25.

13. Carolan, *The Real Cost of Cheap Food,* 103.

14. United States Department of Agriculture. 2015. Turkeys Raised, ISSN: 1949–1972, http://www.nass.usda.gov/Publications/Todays_Reports/reports/tuky0915.pdf, accessed August 11, 2016.

15. Gewertz, Deborah, and Frederick Errington. 2010. *Cheap Meat: Flap Food Nations in the Pacific Islands.* Berkeley, CA: University of California Press.

16. Norris, John. 2013. "Make Them Eat Cake: America Exporting Obesity Epidemic," *Foreign Policy,* September 3, http://www.foreignpolicy.com/articles/2013/09/03/make_them_eat_cake_america_exporting_obesity_epidemic, accessed March 10, 2016.

17. Jang, H. J., Z. Kokrashvili, M. J. Theodorakis, O. D. Carlson, B. J. Kim, J. Zhou, and J. M Egan. 2007. "Gut-Expressed Gustducin and Taste Receptors Regulate Secretion of Glucagon-like Peptide-1," *Proceedings of the National Academy of Sciences* 104 (38): 15069–74.

18. Quoted in: Jones, Eleanor, and Florian Ritzmann. [No date]. "Coca-Cola Goes to War: Coca-Cola at Home," http://xroads.virginia.edu/~class/coke/coke1.html.

19. Ibid.
20. Woolfolk, Mary E., William Castellan, and Charles I. Brooks. 1983. "Pepsi versus Coke: Labels, Not Tastes, Prevail," *Psychological Reports* 52 (1): 185–86.
21. Mirsky, Steve. 2007. "Carrots, Sticks, and Robot Picks," *Scientific American* 297 (4): 48.

Chapter 2

1. Gillette, Mrs. F. L. 1889. *The White House Cookbook.* Chicago, Philadelphia, Stockton, CA: L. P. Miller and Company, unnumbered page.
2. Ibid., 70.
3. "An American Lady." 1864. *The American Home Cook Book.* New York: Dick and Fitzgerald, 22.
4. Ibid.
5. "Kurt," personal interview, December 14, 2014.
6. Tobin, Daniel, Joan Thomson, and Luke LaBorde. 2012. "Consumer Perceptions of Produce Safety: A Study of Pennsylvania," *Food Control* 26 (2): 305–12, 309.
7. Ibid.
8. Vanham, D., F. Bouraoui, A. Leip, B. Grizzetti, and G. Bidoglio. 2015. "Lost Water and Nitrogen Resources Due to EU Consumer Food Waste," *Environmental Research Letters,* 10 (8), http://iopscience.iop.org/article/10.1088/1748-9326/10/8/084008/meta, accessed June 16, 2016.
9. Ibid.
10. Davis, Donald. 2009. "Declining Fruit and Vegetable Nutrient Composition: What Is the Evidence?" *HortScience* 44 (1): 15–19.
11. Estabrook, Barry. 2011. *Tomatoland: How Modern Industrial Agriculture Destroyed Our Most Alluring Fruit.* Kansas City, MO: Andrews McMeel Publishing, 148–49.
12. Davis, "Declining Fruit and Vegetable Nutrient Composition," 19.
13. Jarrell, W., and R. Beverly. 1981. "The Dilution Effect in Plant Nutrition Studies." Pp. 197–224 in *Advances in Agronomy,* Vol. 34, ed. N. C. Brady. New York: Academic Press.
14. Estabrook, *Tomatoland,* 94.
15. Dee, Jon. 2013. "Australia Needs a Food Waste Strategy," ABC.net, June 5,

http://www.abc.net.au/environment/articles/2013/06/05/3774785.htm, accessed February 6, 2016.

16. Hurst, Daniel. 2010. "Growers Go Bananas Over Waste," *Brisbane Times,* January 7, http://www.brisbanetimes.com.au/business/growers-go-banan as-over-waste-20100106-lu7q.html, accessed February 6, 2016.

17. Pimentel, David, and Michael Burgess. 2014. "Environmental and Economic Costs of the Application of Pesticides Primarily in the United States." Pp. 47–71 in *Integrated Pest Management,* ed. David Pimental and Rajinder Peshin. Dordrecht, the Netherlands: Springer Netherlands.

18. In an earlier book, I discuss how eaters need to become tuned to alternative food networks, a concept that appears to have close parallels to Lynn's use of the word *recalibrate.* See: Carolan, M. 2011. *Embodied Food Politics.* Burlington, VT: Ashgate.

19. See, for example: Berger, Peter L., and Thomas Luckmann. 1991 (1966). *The Social Construction of Reality: A Treatise in the Sociology of Knowledge.* London: Penguin.

Chapter 3

1. Franck, Karen. 2005. "The City as Dining Room, Market, and Farm," *Architectural Design* 75 (3): 5–10; Titz, Karl, Je'Anna Lanza-Abbott, and Glenn Cordúa y Cruz. 2004. "The Anatomy of Restaurant Reviews: An Exploratory Study," *International Journal of Hospitality and Tourism Administration* 5 (1): 49–65; Ladhari, Riadh, Isabelle Brun, and Miguel Morales. 2008. "Determinants of Dining Satisfaction and Post-Dining Behavioral Intentions," *International Journal of Hospitality Management* 27 (4): 563–73.

2. See, for example: Alexander, J., T. Crompton, and G. Shrubsole. 2011. "Think of Me as Evil: Opening the Ethical Debates in Advertising," Public Interest Research Centre (PIRC) and WWF-UK, http://assets.wwf.org.uk /downloads/think_of_me_as_evil.pdf, accessed April 6, 2015; Roccas, S., and L. Sagiv. 2010. "Personal Values and Behaviour: Taking the Cultural Context into Account," *Social and Personality Psychology Compass* 4: 30–41.

3. Kasser, Tim. 2002. *The High Price of Materialism.* Cambridge, MA: MIT Press.

4. Kasser, Tim. 2005. "Frugality, Generosity, and Materialism in Children and Adolescents." Pp. 357–73 in *What Do Children Need to Flourish?*

Conceptualizing and Measuring Indicators of Positive Development, ed. K. Moore and L. Lippman. New York: Springer Science.

5. Brown, Kirk, and Tim Kasser. 2005. "Are Psychological and Ecological Well-Being Compatible? The Role of Values, Mindfulness, and Lifestyle," *Social Indicators Research* 74: 349–68.

6. Greenberg, Bradley, and Jeffrey Brand. 1993. "Television News and Advertising in Schools: The 'Channel One' Controversy," *Journal of Communication* 43 (1): 143–51.

7. Good, J. 2007. "Shop 'til We Drop? Television, Materialism, and Attitudes about the Natural Environment," *Mass Communication and Society* 10: 365–83.

8. McLuhan, Marshall. 1964. "The Medium Is the Message." Pp. 23–35, 63–7 in *Understanding Media: The Extensions of Man*. New York: Signet.

9. Carolan, Michael. 2010. "Sociological Ambivalence and Climate Change," *Local Environment* 15 (4): 309–21; Carolan, Michael. 2015. "Affective Sustainable Landscapes and Care Ecologies: Getting a Real Feel for Alternative Food Communities," *Sustainability Science* 10 (2): 317–29.

10. Povey, R., B. Wellens, M. Conner. 2001. "Attitudes towards Following Meat, Vegetarian, and Vegan Diets: An Examination of the Role of Ambivalence," *Appetite* 37: 15–26; Sparks, P., M. Conner, R. James, R. Sheperd, and R. Povey. 2001. "Ambivalence about Health-Related Behaviors: An Exploration in the Domain of Food Choice," *British Journal of Health Psychology* 6: 53–68.

11. Carolan, *The Real Cost of Cheap Food*.

12. Peterson, Anna. 2009. *Everyday Ethics and Social Change: The Education of Desire*. New York: Columbia University Press, 128.

13. See: Niebuhr, Reinhold. 1934. *Moral Man and Immoral Society: A Study in Ethics and Politics*. New York: Charles Scribner's Sons; D'Souza, Albert. 2005. *Christian Ethics and Moral Values*. New Delhi: Mittal Publications.

14. Ingold, Tim. 2000. *The Perception of the Environment: Essays on Livelihood, Dwelling, and Skill*. New York: Routledge, 25.

15. Peterson, Anna. 2009. *Everyday Ethics and Social Change: The Education of Desire*. New York: Columbia University Press.

16. Ibid., 132.

17. Ibid.

18. Linnekin, Baylen. 2016. *Biting the Hand That Feeds Us: How Fewer, Smarter*

Laws Would Make Our Food System More Sustainable. Washington, DC: Island Press.

19. Ibid., 57.

20. Andrew, Smith. 1996. *Pure Ketchup: A History of America's National Condiment, with Recipes.* Columbia, SC: University of South Carolina Press.

21. Rodrik, Dani. 1998. "Why Do More Open Economies Have Bigger Governments?" *Journal of Political Economy* 106 (5): 997.

Chapter 4

1. See: Stephan, Walter G., and Krystina Finlay. 1999. "The Role of Empathy in Improving Intergroup Relations," *Journal of Social Issues* 55 (4): 729–43; Taylor, Charles. 1992. "The Politics of Recognition." Pp. 25–103 in *Multiculturalism and the Politics of Recognition,* ed. Amy Gutmann, Steven C. Rockefeller, Michael Walzer, and Susan Wolf. Princeton NJ: Princeton University Press.

2. Jacobs, Ken. 2015. "Americans Are Spending $153 Billion a Year to Subsidize McDonald's and Wal-Mart's Low-Wage Workers," *Washington Post,* April 15, https://www.washingtonpost.com/posteverything/wp/2015/04/15/we-are-spending-153-billion-a-year-to-subsidize-mcdonalds-and-walmarts-low-wage-workers/, accessed January 4, 2016.

3. See, for example: Gray, Barbara, and Jennifer Kish-Gephart. 2013. "Encountering Social Class Differences at Work: How 'Class Work' Perpetuates Inequality," *Academy of Management Review* 38 (4): 670–99; Kraus, Michael, Paul Piff, Rodolfo Mendoza-Denton, Michelle Rheinschmidt, and Dacher Keltner. 2012. "Social Class, Solipsism, and Contextualism: How the Rich Are Different from the Poor," *Psychological Review* 119: 546–72.

4. Bowles, Samuel, and Herbert Gintis. 2002. "Social Capital and Community Governance," *Economic Journal* 112 (483): F419–36; Malecki, Christine, and Michelle Demaray. 2006. "Social Support as a Buffer in the Relationship between Socioeconomic Status and Academic Performance," *School Psychology Quarterly* 21 (4): 375.

5. Magee, Joe, and Pamela Smith. 2013. "The Social Distance Theory of Power," *Personality and Social Psychology Review* 17 (2): 158–86; Sandel, Michael. 2012. *What Money Can't Buy: The Moral Limits of Markets.* New York: Macmillan.

6. Taylor, Charles. 1992 "The Politics of Recognition." Pp. 25–103 in *Multiculturalism and the Politics of Recognition*, ed. Amy Gutmann, Steven C. Rockefeller, Michael Walzer, and Susan Wolf. Princeton NJ: Princeton University Press.

7. Shogren, J.F., Fox, J.A., Hayes, D.J., and Roosen, J., 1999. Observed choices for food safety in retail, survey, and auction markets. *American Journal of Agricultural Economics, 81(5)*, pp. 1192–1199.

8. (London) *Telegraph*. 2012. "Where Do Milk, Eggs, and Bacon Come From? One in Three Youths Don't Know," June 14, http://www.telegraph .co.uk/foodanddrink/foodanddrinknews/9330894/Where-do-milk-eggs -and-bacon-come-from-One-in-three-youths-dont-know.html, accessed March 24, 2015.

9. See, for example: Carolan, Michael. 2015. "Re-Wilding Food Systems: Visceralities, Utopias, Pragmatism, and Practice." Pp. 126–39 in *Food Utopias: An Invitation to a Food Dialogue*, ed. P. Stock, M. Carolan, and C. Rosin. New York, London: Routledge; Carolan, Michael. 2013. "Putting the 'Alter' in Alternative Food Futures," *New Zealand Sociology* 28 (4): 145–50; Carolan, Michael. 2013. "The Wild Side of Agrifood Studies: On Co-Experimentation, Politics, Change, and Hope," *Sociologia Ruralis* 53 (4): 413–31.

10. See, for example: Carolan, Michael. 2011. *Embodied Food Politics*. Burlington, VT: Ashgate; Obach, Brian, and Kathleen Tobin. 2014. "Civic Agriculture and Community Engagement," *Agriculture and Human Values* 31 (2): 307–22; Pole, Antoinette, and Margaret Gray. 2013. "Farming Alone? What's Up with the 'C' in Community Supported Agriculture?" *Agriculture and Human Values* 30: 85–100.

11. Carolan, Michael. 2016. "More-than-Active Food Citizens: A Longitudinal and Comparative Study of Alternative and Conventional Eaters," *Rural Sociology*, DOI: 10.1111

12. See, for example: Paul, J., and J. Rana. 2012. "Consumer Behavior and Purchase Intention for Organic Food," *Journal of Consumer Marketing* 29 (6): 412–22.

Chapter 5

1. Freedman, David. 2013 "How Junk Food Can End Obesity," *Atlantic Monthly*, July/August, 68–89.

2. Ibid., 80.

3. Ibid.

4. See also: Durie, M. 2004. "Understanding Health and Illness: Research at the Interface between Science and Indigenous Knowledge," *International Journal of Epidemiology* 33 (5): 1138–43.

5. Regarding the Native Americans I spoke with, most were members of the Ute tribe, in addition to two with ties to the Navajo Nation.

6. See, for instance: Mackie, Gareth. 2014. "Fears for Ayrshire Vitamin Plant as DSM Eyes China," *Scotsman,* April 6, http://www.scotsman.com /business/food-drink-agriculture/fears-for-ayrshire-vitamin-plant-as-dsm -eyes-china-1-3366569, accessed April 25, 2015.

7. Bomford, Michael. 2011. *Beyond Food Miles.* Kentucky State University, March 9, http://organic.kysu.edu/BeyondFoodMiles.pdf, accessed September 16, 2016; Carolan, M. 2013. *Reclaiming Food Security.* New York, London: Routledge, 79–80.

8. US Department of Agriculture / US Department of Health and Human Services. 2015. *Scientific Report of the 2015 Dietary Guidelines Advisory Committee,* http://www.health.gov/dietaryguidelines/2015-scientific-report /14-appendix-E2/e2-37.asp, accessed April 27, 2015.

9. See, for instance: Carolan, Michael. *The Real Cost of Cheap Food.*

10. Minter, Adam. 2013. "Coming Your Way: China's Rotten Apples," *Bloomberg View,* September 30, http://www.bloombergview.com/articles /2013-09-30/coming-your-way-china-s-rotten-apples, accessed April 27, 2016.

11. Timmerman, Kelsey. 2013. "Follow Your Labels: American Apple Juice Is a Product of China," *Christian Science Monitor,* July 21, http://www.csmon itor.com/World/Global-Issues/2013/0721/Follow-your-labels-American -apple-juice-is-a-product-of-China, accessed April 27, 2016.

12. Fredman, Roberto. 2014. "How America Fell out of Love with Orange Juice," *Quartz,* February 26, http://qz.com/176096/how-america-fell-out -of-love-with-orange-juice/, accessed April 27, 2015.

13. Hamilton, Alissa. 2010. *Squeezed: What You Didn't Know About Orange Juice.* New Haven, CT: Yale University Press.

14. Beverage Industry. 2012. "State of the Industry: Juice & Juice Drinks," July 18, http://www.bevindustry.com/articles/85660-2012-state-of-the-indus try%E2%80%94juice%E2%80%94juice-drinks, accessed April 26, 2015.

15. Bloomberg. 2013. "Huiyuan Juice to Raise HK$382.5 Million in New-Share Sale," *Bloomberg*, December 5, http://www.bloomberg.com/news/articles/2013-12-04/huiyuan-juice-to-raise-hk-382-5-million-in-new-share-sale, accessed April 26, 2015.

16. Amelinckx, Andrew. 2015. "New Report Tracks Rise of Antibiotic Resistance in Humans and Livestock, *Modern Farmer*," September 17, http://modernfarmer.com/2015/09/cddep-report-antibiotic-resistance, accessed June 30, 2016.

17. Taverinse, Sabrina. 2014. "Antibiotics in Livestock: F.D.A. Finds Use Is Rising," *New York Times*, October 2, http://www.nytimes.com/2014/10/03/science/antibiotics-in-livestock-fda-finds-use-is-rising.html?_r=1, accessed April 26, 2016.

18. Woolhouse, M., M. Ward, B. van Bunnik, and J. Farrar. 2015. "Antimicrobial Resistance in Humans, Livestock, and the Wider Environment," *Philosophical Transactions of the Royal Society B* 370 (1670): 140083.

19. Sato, K., P. Bartlett, R. Erskine, and J. Kaneene. 2005. "A Comparison of Production and Management between Wisconsin Organic and Conventional Dairy Herds," *Livestock Production Science* 93: 105–15, 106.

20. Benbrook, C., et al. 2010. "A Dairy Farm's Footprint: Evaluating the Impacts of Conventional and Organic Farming Systems," The Organic Center, www.organic-center.org/reportfiles/COFEFFinal_Nov_2.pdf, accessed January 31, 2014.

21. Haraway, Donna. 2000. *How Like a Leaf: An Interview with Donna Haraway*. New York: Routledge, 75.

22. Hinchliffe, S., et al. 2012. "Biosecurity and the Topologies of Infected Life: From Borderlines to Borderlands," *Transactions of the Institute of British Geographers* 38: 531–43.

23. Wenner, Melinda. 2007. "Humans Carry More Bacterial Cells than Human Ones," *Scientific American*, November 30, http://www.scientificamerican.com/article/strange-but-true-humans-carry-more-bacterial-cells-than-human-ones/, accessed July 4, 2016.

24. Ibid.

25. Gill, S., et al. 2006. "Metagenomic Analysis of the Human Distal Gut Microbiome," *Science* 312 (5778): 1355–59.

26. Tillisch, K., et al. 2013. "Consumption of Fermented Milk Product with Probiotic Modulates Brain Activity," *Gastroenterology* 144 (7): 1394–401.

27. Centers for Disease Control and Prevention. [No date]. "Estimates of Food-Borne Illness in the United States," https://www.cdc.gov/foodborne burden/, accessed July 1, 2016.

28. Union of Concerned Scientists. [No date]. "Prescription for Trouble: Using Antibiotics to Fatten Livestock," http://www.ucsusa.org/food_and_agricul ture/our-failing-food-system/industrial-agriculture/prescription-for-trou ble.html#.V3b4M5MrKqA, accessed July 1, 2016.

29. Ibid.

30. Wieczorek, K., and J. Osek. 2013. "Antimicrobial Resistance Mechanisms among Campylobacter." *BioMed Research International,* http://dx.doi.org /10.1155/2013/340605.

31. Odegaard, A., W. Koh, J.-M. Yuan, M. Gross, and M. Pereira. 2012. "Western-Style Fast Food Intake and Cardiometabolic Risk in an Eastern Country," *Circulation* 126: 182–88.

32. Kulkarni, S., A. Levin-Rector, M. Ezzati, and C. Murray. 2011. "Falling Behind: Life Expectancy in US Counties from 2000 to 2007 in an International Context," *Population Health Metrics* 9 (1): 1–12.

33. Carolan, Michael. *The Real Cost of Cheap Food.*

34. Pollan, Michael. 2009. "Big Food vs. Big Insurance," *New York Times,* September 9, http://www.nytimes.com/2009/09/10/opinion/10pollan.html? pagewanted=all&_r=0, accessed June 13, 2016.

35. See, for example: Gertel, Jörg, and Sarah Ruth Sippel, eds. 2014. *Seasonal Workers in Mediterranean Agriculture: The Social Costs of Eating Fresh.* New York; London: Routledge.

Chapter 6

1. See: http://www.slowfood.com/, accessed September 19, 2016.

2. Carlo Petrini. 2001. *Slow Food: The Case for Taste.* New York: Columbia University Press, 20.

3. Ibid.

4. See, for example: Rosa, Hartmut. 2005. "The Speed of Global Flows and the Pace of Democratic Politics," *New Political Science* 27 (4): 445–59.

5. Honore, Carl. 2002. "Haste Is Not on the Menu: The Slow Food Movement Considers Itself the Anti-McDonald's," *National Post* 30: B1–2.

6. See, for example: Counihan, Carole. 1999. *The Anthropology of Food and Body: Gender, Meaning, and Power.* New York; London: Routledge.

7. See, for example: http://www.openculture.com/2014/11/michael-pollan -recommends-cooking-books-videos-recipes.html.

8. McIntyre, L., and K. Rondeau. 2011. "Individual Consumer Food Localism: A Review Anchored in Canadian Farmwomen's Reflections," *Journal of Rural Studies* 27 (2): 116–24.

9. According to a USDA working group, "a food desert as a low-income census tract where a substantial number or share of residents has low access to a supermarket or large grocery store. To qualify as low-income, census tracts must meet the Treasury Department's New Markets Tax Credit (NMTC) program eligibility criteria. Furthermore, to qualify as a food desert tract, at least 33 percent of the tract's population or a minimum of 500 people in the tract must have low access to a supermarket or large grocery store." USDA. [No date]. "Definition of a Food Desert," United States Department of Agriculture, Washington, DC, http://www.ers.usda.gov/dataFiles /Food_Access_Research_Atlas/Download_the_Data/Archived_Version/ar chived_documentation.pdf, accessed October 9, 2016.

10. On eating "white," see, for example: Slocum, Rachel. 2007. "Whiteness, Space, and Alternative Food Practice," *Geoforum* 38 (3): 520–33.

11. These questions draw upon: Cresswell, Tim. 2010. "Towards a Politics of Mobility," *Environment and Planning D* 28: 17–31.

12. Cresswell, Tim. 2006. *On the Move: Mobility in the Modern Western World.* New York: Routledge.

13. Montanari, Massimo. 1996. "Beware!" *Slow* 1 (2): 56.

14. Ibid.

Chapter 7

1. Watanabe, T. 2014. "Solutions Sought to Reduce Food Waste at Schools," *Los Angeles Times*, April 1, http://www.latimes.com/local/la-me-lausd-waste -20140402-story.html, accessed November 27, 2015.

2. Georg Christoph Lichtenberg, the eighteenth-century German scientist and satirist, once wrote that "the most dangerous of all falsehoods is a slightly distorted truth" (*The Waste Books*).

3. Just, D., and J. Price. 2013. "Default Options, Incentives, and Food Choices: Evidence from Elementary-School Children," *Public Health Nutrition* 16 (12): 2281–88; Just, D., and J. Price. 2013. "Using Incentives to En-

courage Healthy Eating in Children," *Journal of Human Resources* 48 (4): 855–72.

4. Gneezy, U., S. Meier, and P. Rey-Biel. 2011. "When and Why Incentives (Don't) Work to Modify Behavior," *Journal of Economic Perspectives* 25 (4): 191–210; Kamenica, E. 2012. "Behavioral Economics and Psychology of Incentives," *American Review of Economics* 4 (13): 1–26.

5. See, for example: Titmuss, R. 1970. *The Gift Relationship.* London: Allen and Unwin.

6. Gneezy, U., and A. Rustichini. 2000. "Pay Enough or Don't Pay At All," *Quarterly Journal of Economics* 115 (3): 791–810.

7. North, A., D. Hargreaves, and J. McKendrick. 1997. "In-Store Music Affects Product Choice," *Nature* 390: 132.

8. Vohs, K., N. Mead, and M. Goode. 2006. "The Psychological Consequences of Money," *Science* 314: 1154–56.

9. Rogers, E. 2003. *Diffusion of Innovations.* New York: Free Press, 5.

10. Marisa Michael, personal interview, October 22, 2014.

11. Carolan, Michael. 2016. "More-than-Active Food Citizens: A Longitudinal and Comparative Study of Alternative and Conventional Eaters," *Rural Sociology*, DOI: 10.1111/ruso.12120.

12. Hunt, G., and N. Azrin. 1973. "A Community-Reinforcement Approach to Alcoholism," *Behaviour Research and Therapy* 11: 91–104.

13. See, for example: Lewallen, T., H. Hunt, W. Potts-Datema, S. Zaza, and W. Giles. 2015. "The Whole School, Whole Community, Whole Child Model: A New Approach for Improving Educational Attainment and Healthy Development for Students," *Journal of School Health* 85 (11): 729–39; Flora, C., and A. Gillespie. 2009. "Making Healthy Choices to Reduce Childhood Obesity: Community Capitals and Food and Fitness," *Community Development* 40 (2): 114–22.

Chapter 8

1. Newman, J. 2015. "U.S. Farm Income to Fall to Lowest Levels in Nine Years," *Wall Street Journal,* August 25, http://www.wsj.com/articles/u-s -farm-income-to-fall-to-lowest-level-in-nine-years-1440521337, accessed January 7, 2016.

2. See, for example: Steinmetz, George. 2016. "Super Size: The Dizzying Grandeur of 21st-Century Agriculture," *New York Times,* Oct. 5, http://

www.nytimes.com/interactive/2016/10/09/magazine/big-food-photo-es
say.html?_r=0, accessed October 10, 2016.

3. As quoted in: Rifkin, Jeremy. 2000. *The Age of Access.* New York: Tarcher,
    76.

4. Kelly, K. [No date]. "Access Is Better than Ownership," *Exponential Times,*
    www.exponentialtimes.net/videos/access-better-ownership-0, accessed January 8, 2016.

5. For more about these forms of capital, see, for example: Emery, Mary, and
    Cornelia Flora. 2006. "Spiraling-up: Mapping Community Transformation with Community Capitals Framework," *Community Development* 37
    (1): 19–35; Carolan, Michael, and James Hale. 2016. "'Growing' Communities with Urban Agriculture: Generating Value Above and Below
    Ground," *Community Development* 47 (4): 530–545.

6. See: http://farmhack.org/tools, accessed September 20, 2016.

7. Kitchin, R., and M. Dodge. 2011. *Code/Space: Software and Everyday Life.*
    Cambridge, MA: MIT Press; Carolan, Michael. 2016. "Publicizing Food:
    Big Data, Precision Agriculture, and Co-Experimental Techniques of Addition," *Sociologia Ruralis,* in press, DOI: 10.1111/soru.12120.

Chapter 9

1. Schwartz, Barry. 2004. *The Paradox of Choice: Why More Is Less.* New York:
    Imprint.

2. Roberts, Paul. 2008. *The End of Food.* New York: Houghton Mifflin.

3. North, D. C. 1990. *Institutions, Institutional Change, and Economic Performance.* Cambridge, UK: Cambridge University Press.

4. Hardin, Garrett. 1968. "The Tragedy of the Commons," *Science* 162:
    1243–48.

5. Ibid., 1244.

6. Ibid., 1248.

7. See, for example: Pretty, J., and H. Ward. 2001. "Social Capital and the
    Environment," *World Development* 29 (2): 209–27; Putnam, R. 2001.
    Bowling Alone. New York: Simon & Schuster.

8. See, for example: Orbell, J., A. van de Kragt, and R. Dawes. 1988. "Explaining Discussion-Induced Cooperation in Social Dilemmas," *Journal of
    Personality and Social Psychology* 54: 811–19.

9. Hirschman, Albert. 1970. *Exit, Voice, and Loyalty.* Cambridge, MA: Harvard University Press.

10. Carolan, Michael. 2016. "More-than-Active Food Citizens: A Longitudinal and Comparative Study of Alternative and Conventional Eaters," *Rural Sociology*, DOI: 10.1111.

Index